The War Against Iraq

The War Against Iraq

Other titles in the Lucent Terrorism Library are:

America Under Attack: Primary Sources
America Under Attack: September 11, 2001
The History of Terrorism
Terrorists and Terrorist Groups

THE
LUCENT
TERRORISM
LIBRARY

The War Against Iraq

Debra A. Miller

LUCENT
BOOKS®

THOMSON
™
GALE

San Diego • Detroit • New York • San Francisco • Cleveland • New Haven, Conn. • Waterville, Maine • London • Munich

LIBRARY OF CONGRESS CATALOGING-IN-PUBLICATION DATA

Miller, Debra A.
   The war against Iraq / by Debra A. Miller
     p. cm. — (Terrorism library series:)
Summary: Provides an overview of the 2003 war of the United States and its allies against
Saddam Hussein and Iraq, including historical reasons for the conflict and its political and
economic ramifications.
Includes bibliographical references and index.
   ISBN 1-59018-522-6
   1. Iraq War, 2003—Juvenile literature. [1. Iraq War, 2003.] I. Title. II. Lucent terrorism
library.
   DS79.763.M55 2004
   956.7044'3—dc22

                                                    2003013870

Printed in the United States of America

Contents

FOREWORD   8

INTRODUCTION
  Winning the Peace   10

CHAPTER 1
  Iraq's History of Aggression and Arms   14

CHAPTER 2
  The Axis of Evil and Diplomatic Efforts to Disarm Iraq   28

CHAPTER 3
  Shock and Awe in Twenty-Six Days   43

CHAPTER 4
  The Aftermath of War in Iraq   60

CHAPTER 5
  Challenges for the New Iraq   74

Notes   91
Chronology   95
For Further Reading   98
Works Consulted   100
Index   104
Picture Credits   111
About the Author   112

Foreword

It was the bloodiest day in American history since the battle of Antietam during the Civil War—a day in which everything about the nation would change forever. People, when speaking of the country, would henceforth specify "before September 11" or "after September 11." It was as if, on that Tuesday morning, the borders had suddenly shifted to include Canada and Mexico, or as if the official language of the United States had changed. The difference between "before" and "after" was that pronounced.

That Tuesday morning, September 11, 2001, was the day that Americans began to learn firsthand about terrorism, as first one fuel-heavy commercial airliner, and then a second, hit New York's World Trade Towers—sending them thundering to the ground in a firestorm of smoke and ash. A third airliner was flown into a wall of the Pentagon in Washington, D.C., and a fourth was apparently wrestled away from terrorists before it could be steered into another building. By the time the explosions and collapses had stopped and the fires had been extinguished, more than three thousand Americans had died.

Film clips and photographs showed the horror of that day. Trade Center workers could be seen leaping to their deaths from seventy, eighty, ninety floors up rather than endure the 1,000-degree temperatures within the towers. New Yorkers who had thought they were going to work were caught on film desperately racing the other way to escape the wall of dust and debris that rolled down the streets of lower Manhattan. Photographs showed badly burned Pentagon secretaries and frustrated rescue workers. Later pictures would show huge fire engines buried under the rubble.

It was not the first time America had been the target of terrorists. The same World Trade Center had been targeted in 1993 by Islamic terrorists, but the results had been negligible. The worst of such acts on American soil came in 1995 at the hands of a homegrown terrorist whose hatred for the government led to the bombing of the federal building in Oklahoma City. The blast killed 168 people—19 of them children.

But the September 11 attacks were far different. It was terror on a frighteningly well-planned, larger scale, carried out by nineteen men from the Middle East whose hatred of the United States drove them to the most appalling suicide mission the world had ever witnessed. As one U.S. intelligence officer told a CNN reporter, "These guys turned airplanes into weapons of mass destruction, landmarks familiar to all of us into mass graves."

Some observers say that September 11 may always be remembered as the date that the people of the United States finally came face to face with terrorism. "You've been relatively sheltered from terrorism," says an Israeli terrorism expert. "You hear about it happening here in the Middle East, in Northern Ireland, places far away from you. Now Americans have joined the real world where this ugliness is almost a daily occurrence."

This "real world" presents a formidable challenge to the United States and other nations. It is a world in which there are no rules, where modern terrorism is war not waged on soldiers, but on innocent people—including children. Terrorism is meant to shatter people's hope, to create instability in their daily lives, to make them feel vulnerable and frightened. People who continue to feel unsafe will demand that their leaders make concessions—*do something*—so that terrorists will stop the attacks.

Many experts feel that terrorism against the United States is just beginning. "The tragedy is that other groups, having seen [the success of the September 11 attacks] will think: why not do something else?" says Richard Murphy, former ambassador to Syria and Saudi Arabia. "This is the beginning of their war. There is a mentality at work here that the West is not prepared to understand."

Because terrorism is abhorrent to the vast majority of the nations on the planet, President George W. Bush's declaration of war against terrorism was supported by many other world leaders. He reminded citizens that it would be a long war, and one not easily won. However, as many agree, there is no choice; if terrorism is allowed to continue unchecked the world will never be safe.

The volumes of the Lucent Terrorism Library help to explain the unexplainable events of September 11, 2001, as well as examine the history, personalities, and issues connected with the ensuing war on terror. Annotated bibliographies provide readers with ideas for further research. Fully documented primary and secondary source quotations enliven the text. Each book in this series provides students with a wealth of information as well as launching points for further study and discussion.

Winning the Peace

America's war in Iraq began on March 19, 2003, and was an exercise in overwhelming American firepower and force. Incredibly precise U.S. bombs and missiles struck government targets throughout Iraq, and a stream of American tanks raced toward Baghdad. Although troops faced unexpected resistance along the way and strikes appeared to have failed to kill Saddam Hussein, the bottom line was a quick U.S. victory signaled by the toppling of a huge statue of Saddam Hussein in the center of Baghdad on April 9, only weeks after the war began. The war demonstrated to the world that the United States had the ability to dominate Iraq militarily, sending a warning to other rogue nations that might be acting against U.S. interests. Months later, however, America had yet to convince the world of the rightness of its actions or win the peace in Iraq.

Indeed, the United States led the military attack against Saddam Hussein's regime after a long and fractious international debate, against the will of many of its traditional allies and amid a storm of demonstrations and protests around the world. U.S. president George W. Bush said war was necessary to rid Iraq of weapons of mass destruction, including nuclear, chemical, and biological weapons, and to remove Hussein from power. Ousting Hussein, Bush argued, would remove a dangerous tyrant from the world stage, liberate Iraqis from three decades of Hussein's terror and brutality, and give Iraq a chance to form a free, democratic government.

In the months following the war, however, Iraqis and many others throughout the world remained skeptical that U.S. intentions were based on Iraq's best interests. This skepticism was based on a widely held suspicion that the United States sought to occupy Iraq for its own purposes, perhaps to control Iraqi oil, to profit from doing business with Iraq after the war, or to install a government in Iraq that would be partial to U.S. control. Even before the military operation had ended, some European nations began calling for United Nations (UN) control over the rebuilding of Iraq. The United States also was criticized, even in Britain, when initial rebuilding contracts were swiftly awarded to big American firms that had close connections with President Bush's administration.

Criticism mounted further as U.S. troops failed to provide security in the face of widespread looting and destruction and ethnic clashes between Iraq's three ethnic groups (Sunnis, Shias, and Kurds). To make matters worse, American teams failed to find weapons of mass destruction, the main justification for going to war. Meanwhile, Iraqi demonstrators called the United States an "occupier" instead of a "liberator" and demanded that the U.S. forces leave Iraq immediately, even as Iraqi guerrilla fighters escalated attacks against U.S. troops trying to stabilize the country.

A soldier watches U.S. troops pull down a statue of Saddam Hussein in Baghdad just weeks after the war in Iraq began.

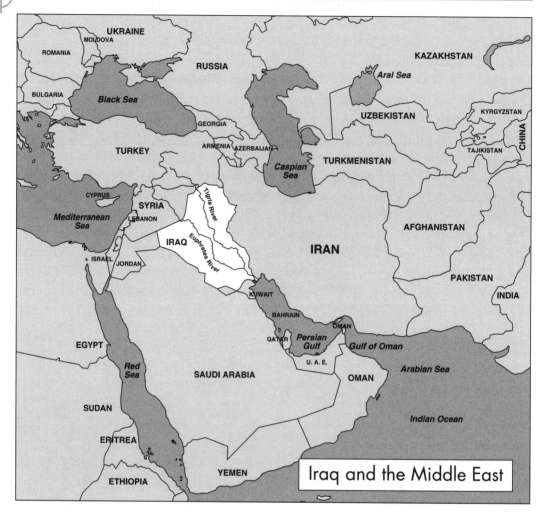

Iraq and the Middle East

The postwar anarchy revealed the short-sighted U.S. focus on war and the stark inadequacy of U.S. postwar nation-building plans and expectations. However, history suggests that these problems, and the difficulty of transforming Iraq into a democracy, should have been anticipated. Indeed, Iraq's history is one marked by political violence, ethnic and religious differences, and exploitation by authoritarian rulers. Today's postwar disorder is merely the twenty-first century's version of this historical pattern.

Similarly, Iraq's tattered economy and infrastructure were wholly predictable, given more than a decade of restrictive UN economic sanctions, the destruction of three wars, and the fallout from almost three decades of terror and thievery by Saddam Hussein and his followers.

Postwar Iraq, therefore, is a mammoth project and one that will likely require many U.S. taxpayer dollars and a long-term commitment of U.S. troops. The challenges for America are daunting. Encouraging quick economic recovery and creating jobs in a broken country, in addition to preventing tribal and ethnic differences from sabotaging the democratic process, are critical to American success. Also important is a resolution of the fate of Saddam Hussein and his followers; if he is not killed or captured, and if Hussein's followers are not completely purged from government and army posts, Iraqis will live in fear that Hussein might regroup in a bid to retake control of Iraq or take revenge against his enemies.

Finally, the United States must overcome the deep distrust of American motives in Iraq. Only by first successfully stabilizing and reconstructing and then by handing over full democratic control to Iraqis will the United States be seen as Iraq's "liberator." And in the end, the true measure of the success or failure of the U.S.-led war will be determined by what kind of government and society emerges in Iraq. As *New York Times* columnist Thomas L. Friedman states, "America's future, and the future of the Mideast, rides on our building a different Iraq."[1]

Chapter One

Iraq's History of Aggression and Arms

Iraq is a young nation that has long suffered from political instability. Only during the last twenty-four years of Saddam Hussein's dictatorship has Iraq achieved a measure of national identity and stability. Yet Hussein failed to use the country's great natural and historical resources to forge a prosperous, free, and peaceful nation. Instead, he employed violence and terror against the Iraqi people and sought to increase his power by building up Iraq's military and by attacking Iraq's neighbors. Iraq's recent history, therefore, became marked by repression, war, and struggles with the international community over weapons of mass destruction.

The British Create Iraq

Iraq is located in an area known in ancient times as Mesopotamia, which means "the land between two rivers,"

the Tigris and the Euphrates. The earliest Arab inhabitants of Mesopotamia were nomadic Arab tribes who wandered the great deserts of the Arabian Peninsula with their caravans of camels. When a new religion called Islam emerged with the birth of the prophet Mohammad in the year A.D. 570, Islam's followers (known as Muslims) established alliances between the various tribes. After the death of Mohammad, the Muslim alliances began to fall apart, but eventually they were replaced by a great Arab empire that spread Islam not only throughout Iraq but also to Syria and Egypt. This Islamic unity, however, was weakened by, among other things, differences that developed between two Muslim sects, the Sunnis and the Shias (also called Shiites), creating a division that continues in Iraq and other places to the present day.

Ancient Mesopotamia

Although Iraq only recently emerged as an independent nation, its history dates back more than five thousand years and contains the world's richest known archaeological sites. Iraq is situated in the land that the ancient Greeks called Mesopotamia, meaning land between the rivers. The name refers to the Tigris and the Euphrates, two large rivers in Iraq. This location became what many have called the "cradle of civilization." On this site in about 4000 B.C. arose the world's first civilization, called Sumer, long before the development of other famous ancient civilizations such as Egypt, Greece, and Rome.

The ancient Sumerians used the fertile land and the abundant water supply of the area to cultivate and irrigate crops, creating the first system of agriculture. In addition, Sumerians are credited with such early human achievements as the invention of writing, the plow, and the wheel. The famous Sumerian city of Ur arose in southern Mesopotamia and became one of the most prosperous Sumerian cities. In about 2340 B.C., however, the Sumerian civilization collapsed after clashes with other peoples who migrated to the Arabian Peninsula.

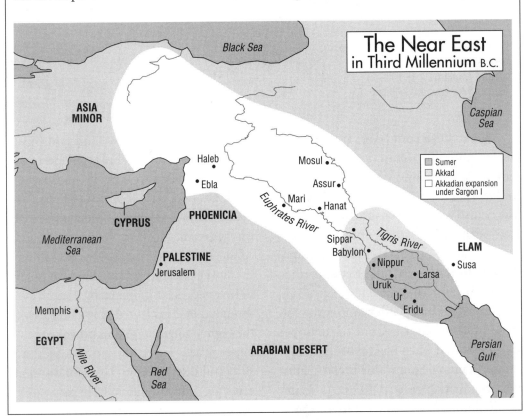

The Near East in Third Millennium B.C.

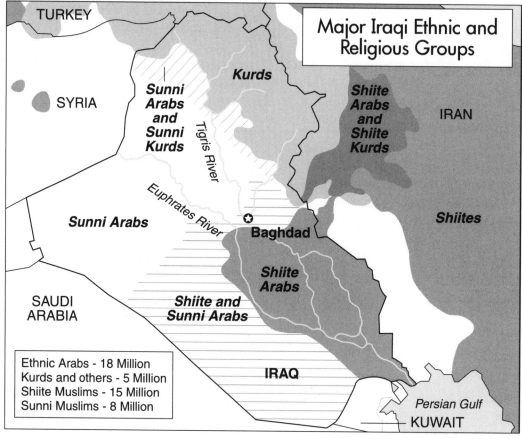

Major Iraqi Ethnic and Religious Groups

TURKEY

SYRIA

Kurds

Sunni Arabs and Sunni Kurds

Shiite Arabs and Shiite Kurds

IRAN

Tigris River

Euphrates River

Sunni Arabs

Baghdad

Shiites

Shiite Arabs

SAUDI ARABIA

Shiite and Sunni Arabs

Ethnic Arabs - 18 Million
Kurds and others - 5 Million
Shiite Muslims - 15 Million
Sunni Muslims - 8 Million

IRAQ

Persian Gulf

KUWAIT

The modern country of Iraq was not created until the twentieth century, when the outbreak of World War I caused Britain to invade areas around Basra and Baghdad. The British wanted to ensure that no other European nation would dominate these areas because such a development might threaten their route to India, a country then part of Britain's colonial empire. Arabs in Iraq hoped for independence after the collapse of Ottoman rule, but these hopes were destroyed when Britain brutally suppressed a united Sunni-Shia revolt against postwar British rule in 1920. As writer Geoff Simons describes, "Punitive expedi-

tions were launched by land and by air against the tribes: whole villages were destroyed by British artillery and suspected ringleaders were shot without trial."[2] In 1921 Britain imposed a colonial monarchy on the area headed by a Syrian, King Faisal, of the Sunni faith.

Due to Britain's actions, the government in Iraq became dominated by Sunnis, even though they constituted only a minority of the population in Iraq. This provoked more tensions between Sunni and Shia Muslims. Britain also set the boundaries for the modern state of Iraq artificially, in response to Western interests and in order to control sites of Iraqi oil reserves. These boundaries included not only Arab-populated areas but also an area near Turkey inhabited by a non-Arab ethnic group of Indo-European ancestry called the Kurds, whose culture and history is separate from both the Sunnis and the Shias. This artificial grouping of three distinct ethnic sects in the same country deepened ethnic differences.

Indeed, the British policies in Iraq only worsened the historical ethnic divisions and violence that had plagued the area since ancient times. As journalist Said K. Aburish explains,

> Just as the long-term history of Iraq contained and nurtured violence, the British, following short-sighted policies similar to those employed by Iraq's ancient conquerors, contributed measurably to the ethnic, religious and social divisions which beset the country.[3]

Iraq became a sovereign state in 1932 but continued to suffer from political unrest caused by opposition to British control and conflict between Iraq's three ethnic sects—Sunnis, Shias, and Kurds.

The Rise of Saddam Hussein

In 1958 the British monarchy in Iraq was overthrown in a coup led by a military officer, Abdul Karim Qasim. Qasim's revolution won the support of most Iraqis and succeeded in ridding Iraq of remnants of British repression. However, when the new government adopted Communist social and economic reforms that were unpopular with many Sunnis (who wanted Iraq to become friendly with Egypt, an Arab country that opposed Communist policies), Qasim was unable to hold onto power. He was overthrown in 1963 by the Baath Party, a pro-Arab political group that included in its membership a young Saddam Hussein. Many believe that the Baath Party was aided in the coup by the U.S. Central Intelligence Agency (CIA) in order to ensure that a pro-Western government ruled Iraq.

Although the Baath Party was quickly overtaken nine months later in another coup by military officers, it regained power in 1968. This time, the party was more organized, led by a group of Sunni Arabs from the Iraqi town of Tikrit who were united by tribal and family ties. Saddam Hussein was part of this Sunni tribe from Tikrit. Indeed, his cousin was Ahmad Hasan al-Bakr, the respected military leader who became president of the Baath Party's new government in Iraq, giving Hussein access to the highest levels of power. Hussein soon became a key figure in the Baath Party, second in power only to President Bakr.

Although the new Baath government claimed its rule was the will of the Iraqi people, in reality its policies created, as author Geoff Simons describes, "one-party rule supported by a network of terrorist organizations used to suppress all political opposition . . . [creating] a system of state terror to discourage any potential threats to the regime."[4] For many years Hussein operated behind the scenes as the ruthless commander of this Baath Party security system, helping the party to establish a repressive dictatorship throughout Iraq.

Saddam Hussein's Reign of Terror

Saddam Hussein, after gaining power in Iraq, increased the activities of his security force and used terror and torture against anyone who dared criticize or threaten his regime. During Hussein's rule, for example, Iraqi law provided for twenty-four political crimes punishable by death that fell under the heading of treason. Also, as newspaper editor and Middle East expert Con Coughlin has noted in his book, *Saddam: King of Terror*, "The definition of these capital offenses was deliberately vague so that any unauthorized disclosure of information could be interpreted as treason." This allowed the security forces unlimited power to act for virtually any reason against almost anyone, including women and children.

Those who became the victims of this regime of terror faced not only beatings and sometimes execution, but also horrible forms of torture. As Coughlin describes, the regime had 107 different methods of torturing its enemies, including:

> Manual torture took the form of beatings, hair pulling, bastinado (beating with a stick on the soles of the feet), and the twisting of limbs until they broke. Electric shocks were commonly applied to extract confessions, and a wide range of psychological torture was also implemented. The standard

form of torture was to place the victims in solitary confinement for long periods. Some prisoners were left in cold cells until their limbs froze, while on other occasions parts of the prisoners' bodies were set on fire. Another particular Iraqi specialty was to rape relatives of those detained—male and female—while the accused were forced to watch. Saddam's torturers could also make use of a variety of machines that were available for removing human limbs, from fingers to legs.

Hussein's government also was characterized by complete government control of the media, the court system, and every other Iraqi institution and department. There was no freedom of expression and all newspapers, radio, and television were used instead as instruments for Baath Party propaganda. Indeed, Saddam Hussein was glorified by the state-controlled media and used to build a cult around him as Iraq's great leader. As a group of Iraqis living in exile wrote in a memo to the United Nations, quoted in Coughlin's book: "The dictatorship of Saddam Hussein is one of the harshest, most ruthless and most unscrupulous regimes in the world. It is a totalitarian, one-party system based on the personality cult of Saddam Hussein."

His first step in this role was to execute fourteen men that the Baath Party did not trust, accusing them of being part of an Israeli spy network. Hussein then continued to purge all others who might threaten the power of the party, using tactics of brutality and terror that have become legendary. To give just one example, author Geoff Simons recounts a report from someone who witnessed Hussein in action:

Saddam Hussein addresses a crowd after the 1969 hanging of fourteen Iraqis whom the Baath Party accused of spying for Israel.

"[Saddam] came into the room, picked up [his victim] and dropped him into a bath of acid. And then he watched while the body dissolved."[5] Other terror tactics used by Hussein against persons he viewed as traitors included other forms of execution and assassination, imprisonment, exile, and torture.

Saddam's Power Grows

As time progressed, Saddam Hussein's power grew. In addition to continuing his focus on security and terror, he increased membership of the Baath Party and surrounded himself with a network of loyal family members by appointing them to positions of importance. He also created his own Popular Army in order to lessen the regular army's power. At the same time, he became involved in social and economic issues such as land reform and health care, gaining recognition for his concerns for the poor. He also used propaganda to increase

19

his popularity, publicizing flattering pictures of himself with his family and using radio and television to reach ordinary people with these types of positive images. In addition, Hussein became involved in major issues such as Kurdish rebellions, Shia opposition to the Baath regime, and Iraqi oil. Indeed, as Geoff Simon notes, "Throughout the 1970s and after, Saddam Hussein was a principal architect of Iraqi policies."[6]

Hussein's handling of some of these thorny issues demonstrated his superior political and manipulative skills. For example, although he generously granted the Kurds substantial concessions and promised them autonomy in 1970, he soon thereafter began to evict Kurds from their lands and tried to assassinate their leaders, leading the Kurds to seek support from Iran. After years of fighting between the Kurds and the Iraqi government, Hussein in 1975 suppressed the Kurdish uprising by negotiating an agreement with Iran that cut off vital Iranian support for the Kurds. Similarly,

Saddam Hussein, right, meets with a Kurdish leader. Throughout the 1970s, Hussein evicted the Kurds from their land and tried to assassinate their leaders.

Hussein assumed responsibilities for negotiating with the Iraqi Petroleum Company (IPC), a group of international oil companies (including Shell, Esso, Mobil, British Petroleum, and Compagnie Francaise des Petroles) that controlled development of Iraqi oil. He ultimately succeeded in nationalizing the IPC in 1972, giving ownership of Iraqi oil to Iraq and declaring in popular radio messages that "Arab Oil [is] for the Arabs."[7]

Finally, in 1979, Hussein seized the presidency of Iraq from Bakr, and immediately carried out a terror purge of the party to eliminate all opposition and establish his complete control of Iraq. At a closed session of the Baath Party's Revolutionary Command Council on July 17, 1979, for example, Hussein slowly and dramatically read the names of those whom he accused of plots against Iraq; those named were then led out of the room to eventually face firing squads formed from the surviving members of the council. At this point, as Geoff Simons notes, "there was no one left to challenge Saddam's authority,"[8] and Iraq was fully under his control.

Both before and after attaining the presidency, Hussein used Iraq's valuable oil wealth (estimated at $21.3 billion in 1980) to strengthen his army and implement economic development programs that improved health, education, agriculture, and housing. These economic incentives allowed many Iraqis to rise to middle-class status and created popular support for Saddam Hussein's regime. The economic improvements also succeeded in uniting Iraq's three disparate groups (Sunnis, Shias, Kurds) more than ever before in Iraq's history. Despite his brutality, therefore, Hussein created stability and some measure of national identity for Iraq.

Iraq's War Against Iran

With his regime secure at home, Hussein next sought to increase his power in the Arab world and on the international stage. His first action in this new direction came in 1980, when Iraq attacked Iran.

Although Iran and Iraq had a history of rivalry, a serious dispute began in 1979, when the Islamic Revolution in Iran stirred up anti-Baath sentiments among Iraq's Shia Muslims, who had been long excluded from political or economic power in Iraq despite their majority status. As early as the mid-1970s, Iraqi Shias, united by a Muslim group called Al Daawa al Islamiya (meaning the Islamic Call), began to openly demonstrate against the Baathist regime. Saddam Hussein, realizing the threat to his rule, responded by banning the Daawa Party and executing Daawa leaders.

However, when the Ayatollah Khomeni, a powerful Shia, came to power in Iran, Iraq's Shia population was reinvigorated, as Iran provided them with training and encouragement. For example, Khomeni openly declared in April 1980, "the people and army of Iraq must turn their backs on the Ba'ath regime and overthrow it."[9] After numerous border skirmishes between the two countries, Iraq attacked Iran on September 22, 1980, leading to a protracted seven-year war.

Casualties of the Iran-Iraq War litter a rocky hillside. The war lasted for seven years and resulted in the loss of more than 360,000 lives.

The Iraqi army, however, was unable to defeat Iran, and by 1982 Iraq was on the defensive militarily. Eventually, fears about the revolutionary, fundamentalist Islamic government in Iran caused many countries to come to Iraq's aid. Neighboring Arab nations such as Kuwait and Saudi Arabia lent their support, and the Soviet Union and European nations such as France and Britain provided arms to Iraq. Although the United States initially provided arms to Iran, U.S. policy eventually shifted in favor of Iraq. Over the course of the war, the United States provided billions of dollars of military support and surveillance information to Iraq, including materials to help Iraq develop chemical and biological weapons.

The Iran-Iraq War ended through a United Nations–sponsored ceasefire and resolution accepted in 1988. The war thus produced no victory for either side but cost approximately 367,000 lives and resulted in massive economic destruction for both countries. Iraq emerged from the war crippled economically but with a strong military and chemical weapons, which Hussein used both against Iran during the war and in Iraq against Kurdish civilians in 1987 and 1988. The war, therefore, strengthened Saddam Hussein's regime and turned Iraq into a formidable military power. As Mideast expert Con Coughlin reports, "by 1988, Iraq had developed the fourth largest army in the world."[10]

Iraq's Attack on Kuwait

After the war with Iran, Saddam Hussein wanted to revive the Iraqi economy. At the same time, he continued to build up the country's military, including chemical, biological, and nuclear weapons. He depended on profits from Iraqi oil to do both, even though much of the oil income had to go first to repay war debts. As a result, Iraq's economy continued to struggle, and in 1990 Hussein began to pressure Kuwait and Saudi Arabia to write off Iraqi debts incurred during the Iran-Iraq War. In May 1990 Hussein became concerned that over-

production of oil was depressing oil prices. He accused Kuwait of flooding the market in violation of OPEC (Organization of Petroleum Exporting Countries) production quotas, causing a drop in Iraq's oil revenues at a time when Hussein could least afford it. Hussein also nursed long-held grievances against Kuwait concerning two areas claimed historically by Iraq—oil fields in Rumeila, an area on the border between the two countries, and two islands overlooking one of Iraq's two ports to the gulf. He demanded that Kuwait reduce oil production, write off Iraqi debts, and help pay for Iraq's reconstruction.

Other Arab countries sought to mediate the dispute, but this failed as Iraq invaded Kuwait on August 2, 1990, and quickly seized control of the country. However, as writer and Mideast expert Con Coughlin explains, "Saddam's invasion of Kuwait will be remembered as one of the great military miscalculations of modern history,"[11] because the United Nations Security Council immediately responded with a unanimous resolution condemning the invasion and demanding Iraq's withdrawal. Most Arab nations also condemned Iraq, and then-U.S. president George H.W. Bush called the invasion an "outrageous and brutal act of aggression."[12]

The Gulf War

Saddam Hussein's refusal to withdraw from Kuwait had profound consequences for Iraq. The United States put together a coalition within the UN that included not only traditional European allies but also Turkey,

Saudi Arabia, and other Arab nations. The UN imposed economic sanctions, which placed strict limits on the country's exports and imports and were aimed at forcing Hussein to withdraw and disarm. When Hussein did not leave Kuwait, a massive military attack called Operation Desert Storm was authorized by the United Nations and launched by the United States and its allies on January 16, 1991.

The attack, as writer Con Coughlin describes, "subjected Iraq to one of the most intensive aerial bombardments known to the modern world."[13] Despite its large air force and air defenses, Iraq could not match the allied air power, leaving Iraqi targets ripe for allied bombings and a later ground assault. As a result, what became known as the Gulf War lasted only a few short months and accomplished its stated goals of

People celebrate the liberation of Kuwait City in February 1991. The Gulf War ended quickly, as the allies easily overpowered Saddam Hussein's Iraqi army.

destroying most of Iraq's military arsenal (including nuclear and chemical facilities) and liberating Kuwait. However, the war also destroyed much of Iraq's urban infrastructure, including irrigation, water, and sewage systems, causing lack of clean water, disease, and food shortages. The effects of the war would be felt by the Iraqi people throughout the 1990s.

UN Arms Inspections and Sanctions in the 1990s

After the war the United Nations voted to keep sanctions in place until all of Iraq's weapons of mass destruction (WMD) programs were destroyed. A weapons inspection team, called the United Nations Special Commission on Iraq (UNSCOM), was assembled to monitor the disarming, and in the years that followed, UNSCOM uncovered and destroyed much of Iraq's WMD arsenal. Saddam Hussein, however, made the disarmament effort as difficult as possible by blocking access, lying about the extent or existence of weapons programs, and generally obstructing the UN team. Indeed, according to a background paper produced by the administration of President George W. Bush, Hussein during this period "repeatedly violated sixteen United Nations Security Council Resolutions designed to ensure that Iraq [did] not pose a threat."[14]

Slowly, Hussein managed to weaken the weapons inspections. For example, in 1997 he declared several sites to be "presidential" and negotiated with the United Nations to respect Iraq's sovereignty at those sites.

Hussein later further restricted inspections, accusing the United States of using UNSCOM as a vehicle for spying on Iraq. This led to a suspension of weapons inspections in 1998.

The economic sanctions on Iraq, however, were continued by the UN despite their heavy burden on the Iraqi economy and population. The sanctions created in 1990 prohibited UN member states from importing goods made in Iraq and from selling products to Iraq. UN members also were disallowed from investing in any Iraqi economic activities. Exceptions were made for humanitarian items such as certain food and medial supplies, but these exceptions were very limited and did not include many items considered necessary by Iraqis, such as clothes, shoes, blankets, spare parts for water treatment and sewage disposal, educational materials, and similar items.

Indeed, many criticized the sanctions on humanitarian grounds, arguing that they caused unjustified suffering for the Iraqi people, without hurting Saddam Hussein. No one can deny that sanctions devastated the Iraqi economy, impoverished the middle class, and created severe health and food crises. Also, as many as five hundred thousand Iraqi children are estimated to have died as a result of sanctions. The United Nations tried to respond to these humanitarian problems by authorizing an oil-for-food program under which Iraq was allowed to sell oil to purchase food, medicine, and other necessities. The program helped a bit to ease the effect of sanctions, but in many cases Saddam Hussein refused to purchase humanitarian items for his people, preferring instead to sell oil illegally to acquire money to build new palaces and pay for luxuries for supporters of his regime. Most agree, however, that the sanctions limited to some degree Hussein's ability to import items that could be used to produce conventional as well as nuclear and biological weapons.

The United States, during the years following Iraq's attack on Kuwait, maintained a military presence in and around Iraq and repeatedly conducted air and missile strikes on Iraqi targets. The goals of these military efforts varied—to restrict Iraqi military movements and aggression, to respond to Iraqi incursions into no-fly zones (areas in the north and south where Iraq was not permitted to fly), to repel Iraqi aggression against the Kurds (Operation Desert Strike in 1996), or in retaliation for Iraq's defiance over weapons inspections (Operation Desert Fox in 1998). Some argued, however, that, unlike the initial strike on Iraq in 1991, which was authorized by the United Nations, the United States conducted these

UN weapons inspectors oversee the destruction of Iraqi biological weapons in 1996. Throughout the 1990s, Saddam Hussein thwarted the efforts of UN inspectors.

later military strikes on its own initiative and illegally. Indeed, in the years following the Kuwait invasion, the United States often found itself alone on issues relating to Iraq, without the support of allies in Europe or the Arab states.

To a limited extent the United States also explored the possibilities of encouraging opposition groups within Iraq to overthrow Saddam Hussein, with not much success. Hussein's tight security within his regime and the lack of substantial aid from the United States made a coup against the Iraqi government very unlikely. In addition, the United States failed to support the most promising uprising against Hussein in decades. In 1991, at the end of Desert Storm, with encouragement from U.S. president Bush, Iraqi Shias revolted in southern Iraq; the United States failed to intervene or provide aid, however, and Saddam Hussein crushed the rebellion, killing thousands.

At the beginning of the twenty-first century, more than ten years after Saddam Hussein invaded Kuwait, his country lay in ruins, his people were starving, his economy was shattered, and his military was almost destroyed. Yet he had managed to halt weapons inspections and weaken sanctions. He had watched the broad coalition of nations that attacked him in 1991 fall apart. No opposition groups had overthrown him. His regime had survived, and many feared that he was once again developing weapons of mass destruction, including nuclear weapons and the missiles to launch them.

Chapter Two

The Axis of Evil and Diplomatic Efforts to Disarm Iraq

Many countries believed that Saddam Hussein remained a military threat even after more than a decade of efforts by the United States and the United Nations to disarm Iraq. Yet as of 2001 UN weapons inspections remained indefinitely suspended, and there was no clear international plan for how to make sure that Iraq was disarmed. The September 11, 2001, terrorist attacks on the United States finally provided the impetus for a U.S. drive for war against Iraq. This time, however, unlike the 1991 Gulf War, U.S. goals included not only disarming Iraq but also toppling the regime of Saddam Hussein.

September 11, 2001, and the War on Terrorism

The September 11, 2001, terrorist attack by the terrorist group al-Qaeda proved to be the turning point for American policies on terrorism. Shortly after the terrorist attack, on September 20, 2001, U.S. president George Bush declared war on terrorism in an address to Congress and the nation, promising to use every resource and tool, even war, to disrupt and defeat the global terror network. In addition, Bush signaled a U.S. intention to conduct a military strike on countries that harbor terrorists or support terrorism:

> We will pursue nations that provide aid or safe haven to terrorism. Every nation, in every region, now has a decision to make. Either you are with us, or you are with the terrorists. From this day forward, any nation that continues to harbor or support terrorism will be regarded by the United States as a hostile regime.[15]

The south tower of the World Trade Center explodes after being struck by an airplane on September 11, 2001. This attack changed the way the American government dealt with terrorism.

do so, and as a result, on October 7, 2001, the United States and Britain attacked Afghanistan. Over the next few months U.S. and British forces ousted the Taliban regime and destroyed al-Qaeda bases there.

The U.S. Push for Action Against Iraq

Following the successful military action against Afghanistan, U.S. president George W. Bush praised the U.S. military victory in his State of the Union address to the nation on January 29, 2002. In the same speech Bush warned of another facet of terrorism—an "axis of evil" consisting of three countries: Iraq, Iran, and North Korea. He charged that these states sponsor terrorism and seek to develop chemical, biological, and nuclear weapons:

States like these, and their terrorist allies, constitute an axis of evil, arming to threaten the peace of the world. By seeking weapons of mass destruction, these regimes pose a grave and growing danger. They could provide these arms to terrorists, giving them the means to match their hatred. They could attack our allies or attempt

President Bush delivers his 2002 State of the Union address in which he labeled Iraq, Iran, and North Korea an "axis of evil."

This pledge quickly became a reality. Shortly after Bush's speech the United States accused Afghanistan's Taliban government of harboring terrorists and demanded that it turn over al-Qaeda terrorists to the United States and close all terrorist bases in the country. The Taliban regime refused to

to blackmail the United States. In any of these cases, the price of indifference would be catastrophic.[16]

Regarding Iraq the president charged that the Iraqi regime had plotted to develop anthrax and nerve gas and nuclear weapons for over a decade, had already used chemical weapons to murder thousands of its own citizens, and "is a regime that has something to hide from the civilized world."[17] Bush suggested that military action might be used by the United States in the near future, stating,

> We'll be deliberate, yet time is not on our side. I will not wait on events, while dangers gather. I will not stand by, as peril draws closer and closer. The United States of America will not permit the world's most dangerous regimes to threaten us with the world's most destructive weapons.[18]

Soon after the speech, members of President Bush's administration began openly threatening war with Iraq and advocating Hussein's removal from power. Defense Department officials Richard Perle and Paul Wolfowitz, for example, argued that the only way to prevent Iraq from developing or using weapons of mass destruction was to use military force to overthrow Saddam Hussein and install a pro–U. S. government. Others in the Bush administration emphasized that it was important to remove Hussein from power quickly, before he was able to fully develop his weapons of mass destruction capabilities. In a speech given to the Veterans of Foreign Wars on August 26, 2002, for example, Vice President Dick Cheney warned,

> Armed with an arsenal of these weapons of terror, and seated atop ten percent of the world's oil reserves, Saddam Hussein could then be expected to seek domination of the entire Middle East, take control of a great portion of the world's energy supplies, directly threaten America's friends throughout the region, and subject the United States or any other nation to nuclear blackmail.[19]

Opposition to Bush's Views of the Iraqi Threat

The president, however, faced stiff opposition to his proposal for military action against Iraq. The opposition came from many different quarters, both inside and outside his administration, and from both Democrats and Republicans. His critics pointed out that there was no evidence that Hussein possessed nuclear or missile capabilities that would pose a current or imminent threat to the United States. Indeed, in testimony before the Senate Foreign Relations Committee on July 31, 2002, Richard Butler, the former head of UNSCOM, the team of weapons inspectors that searched for weapons in Iraq during the 1990s, noted the lack of knowledge about the status of Iraq's weapons of mass destruction, stating:

> We do not know and never have known fully the quantity and quality of Iraq's WMD [weapons of mass destruction].

U.S. Evidence of Iraq's Weapons of Mass Destruction

On February 5, 2003, U.S. secretary of state Colin Powell spoke at the United Nations to present information that the United States knew about Iraq's weapons of mass destruction and to try to persuade UN member countries to support a military action against Iraq. Powell reminded UN members that Iraq admitted having vast quantities of biological weapons in 1995, was known to have used chemical weapons against the Kurds in 1988, and in both 1991 and 1995 was discovered to have been working on developing nuclear weapons. He argued that Iraq had failed to account for many of these weapons as the UN demanded, and had been trying to conceal evidence of pro-

hibited weapons from UN weapons inspectors. The evidence Powell presented included audio tapes of discussions between Iraqi military officers allegedly discussing how to hide prohibited items from UN weapons inspectors, satellite photos of a weapons munition and missile facilities allegedly showing trucks used for decontaminating and moving prohibited materials just prior to visits by UN weapons inspectors, and a large engine test stand used by Iraq for testing prohibited long-range ballistic missiles.

In addition, Powell presented information from human sources stating that Saddam Hussein had warned all Iraqi scientists of the serious consequences that they and their families would face if they revealed any sensitive information to the inspectors and that Iraq had been experimenting on human beings to perfect its biological or chemical weapons. Further evidence presented came from Iraqi defectors stating that Iraq had mobile production facilities used to make biological agents and that Hussein had made repeated attempts to acquire high-specification aluminum tubes from eleven different countries, for use in making nuclear weapons.

In a 2003 presentation at the UN, Colin Powell presented satellite photos like this one as evidence of Iraq's weapons program.

May 2002

Decontamination Vehicle

Forklift

35-Ton Cargo Trucks

Its policies of concealment ensured this. …What [Iraq] has been able to further achieve in the four years without inspection is not clear, in precise terms.[20]

Given the lack of firm information about weapons of mass destruction, critics of a war plan suggested that the United States wanted war with Iraq not to counter a threat from such weapons, but instead to remove Hussein and install a U.S.-friendly government in Iraq. This, they said, would ensure U.S. access to Iraqi oil reserves, which are the second largest in the world and constitute a significant portion of U.S. oil imports.

Others questioned what was viewed as a new Bush policy of "preemption," referring to U.S. preventative action against countries that pose no present threat but may, at some time in the future, threaten U.S. interests. Bush said that the new policy was necessary to remove terrorist threats, but critics argued that it reversed previous U.S. efforts to limit military action to defensive purposes. This, critics said, could be very dangerous because it gives the United States license to attack other countries and could lead other countries to adopt similar aggressive policies against the United States or other nations.

Still others worried that there was no plan to stabilize Iraq after Hussein was removed from power. The cost of a war and the aftermath, they said, would be astronomical for the United States.

Iraq's Link to Terror

Many opponents of Bush's proposed war on Iraq pointed out that there was no link between Iraq and terrorists. Indeed, in the days after the September 11 terrorist attack, even the U.S. secretary of state, Colin Powell, admitted that he could find "no clear link"[21] between Osama bin Laden and Saddam Hussein. The CIA continued to maintain this position for many months. However, President Bush and his backers eventually began to claim there was such a connection. First, their claims centered around an alleged meeting in Prague, Czechoslovakia, in April 2001 between the leader of the September 11 hijackers, Mohamed Atta, and an Iraqi intelligence agent. After an investigation, however, the Czechs concluded that the report could not be substantiated.

Next, the Bush administration pointed to an al-Qaeda terrorist camp in northern Iraq that was providing a haven for a terrorist known as Abu Musaab al-Zarqawi, allegedly a senior al-Qaeda leader who escaped from Afghanistan into Iraq and was treated at a Baghdad hospital. Although there was no proof, Bush and his team claimed that Hussein's secret police most certainly knew of al-Zarqawi's presence, thus establishing that Iraq was harboring terrorists. Bush himself made this claim in an October 7, 2002, speech to the nation. However, there were credible reports that al-Zarqawi had left Iraq, that he was not part of al-Qaeda, and that Iraq had no control over or relationship with him. Bush's critics claimed that this evidence, at best, established a very weak connection between Iraq and terrorism.

In addition opponents of the war plan argued that diverting resources to fight Iraq

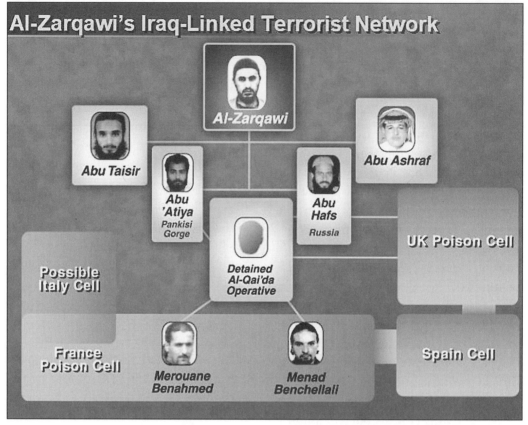

Al-Zarqawi's Iraq-Linked Terrorist Network

Al-Zarqawi

Abu Taisir

Abu 'Atiya
Pankisi Gorge

Abu Ashraf

Abu Hafs
Russia

UK Poison Cell

Detained Al-Qai'da Operative

Possible Italy Cell

France Poison Cell

Merouane Benahmed

Menad Benchellali

Spain Cell

A State Department slide shows the terrorist network headed by al-Qaeda leader Abu Musaab al-Zarqawi, whom the Bush administration believes sought refuge in Iraq.

could actually detract from America's war on terror. In September 2002, for example, Al Gore, vice president during President Bill Clinton's administration and the Democratic nominee for president in 2000, spoke out against military action in Iraq, stating, "I am deeply concerned that the policy we are presently following with respect to Iraq has the potential to seriously damage our ability to win the war against terrorism and to weaken our ability to lead the world in this new century."[22] Gore explained that U.S. action against Iraq without broad support could hurt the broad international cooperation necessary for the war against terror.

U.S. Criticized for Going It Alone

Finally, many of America's European and Arab allies were not on board with the United States for any sort of military action against Iraq. Important members of the UN Security Council, the group of UN members who have the power to obligate the UN, opposed a U.S. invasion of Iraq. Russia, Germany, and France, for example, wanted to see a diplomatic solution. Only Tony Blair, prime minister of Britain, stood squarely behind the U.S. position. "Also, as noted by David Gergen, a special adviser to President Bill Clinton and White House staff member in previous administrations, the Arab world was strongly opposed" to any action against Iraq because of possible anti-American uprisings: "Closer to Iraq, almost every country says don't go; they are more worried about bedlam on their streets than about threats by Saddam."[23]

European leaders made their opposition to a U.S. military strike especially clear. French president Jacques Chirac, for example, in a September 9, 2002, interview, urged the United States not to go it alone and to consult with the United Nations Security Council concerning any military action against Saddam Hussein:

I am totally against unilateralism [nations taking action alone] in the modern world. I believe that the modern world must be coherent and consequently, if a military action is to be undertaken, it must be the responsibility of the international community, via a decision by the [UN] Security Council.[24]

Chirac argued that weapons inspectors must be returned to Iraq and that changing the government of Iraq was not authorized by the United Nations.

Bush Tries Diplomacy

President Bush initially appeared to respond to the pressure from European nations such as France and Britain for diplomacy and cooperation with the UN to contain the Iraqi threat. On September 12, 2002, in a much-anticipated address to the United Nations, Bush asked for UN help and for renewed weapons inspections in Iraq. In the speech Bush set forth his case against Saddam Hussein, citing Iraq's failure to disarm, as required by numerous UN resolutions, and the four-year opportunity Iraq had to rebuild its weapons arsenals since UN inspectors were last allowed into Iraq. He concluded,

We know that Saddam Hussein pursued weapons of mass murder even when inspectors were in the country. Are we to assume that he stopped when they left? The history, the logic and the facts lead to one conclusion. Saddam Hussein's regime is a grave and gathering danger.[25]

The president insisted that Iraq disarm, stop its support for terrorism, cease persecution of Iraqi civilians, resolve issues of unaccounted-for Gulf War personnel, and end illicit trade that violated economic sanctions. Finally, Bush urged the United Nations to develop a resolution to combat the Iraqi threat.

Bush's UN speech was immediately praised by European and some Arab countries, as well as domestically, and U.S. diplomats began working with other countries to develop the appropriate UN resolution to renew weapons inspections. Meanwhile, Bush and his British ally, Tony Blair, continued to warn about the dangers of Iraq.

Antiwar Protests in America and Abroad

The opposition the United States faced at the UN, in large part, reflected antiwar sentiments of people around the world. Not only in Europe, but also in Asian, South American, and Arab countries, hundreds of peace rallies were held denouncing the U.S. rush to war. Indeed, even in the United States, antiwar protests drew some of the largest crowds in years. Weekend marches in mid-February, for example, were especially large, drawing many millions of people to the streets around the globe, particularly in Europe. Protesters that weekend in Britain were estimated at 2 million, in Spain 2 million, in Italy 1 million, in Germany half a million, and in France 300,000. In New York City alone, crowds numbered more than 375,000, and many more Americans protested in other U.S. cities and small towns. Thousands more protested in other countries, such as Ireland, Greece, Russia, and Turkey.

The protests were deemed historic—the largest antiwar demonstrations in history. Antiwar protesters chanted "No war with Iraq" and carried signs with slogans such as "Bush only wants oil" and "No to Bushery." Many of the protesters in the United States were part of organized antiwar coalitions, including United for Peace, an umbrella group of more than 120 organizations, and Win Without War, a coalition of religious, business, and civic leaders. These groups won support from groups such as labor unions, which donated both money and personnel that helped to organize the marches. Other protesters were simply individual citizens fed up with the policies of President Bush.

Demonstrators gather in London, England, in February 2003 to protest the war in Iraq.

A representative delivers Iraq's weapons declaration to UN officials in December 2002. UNMOVIC chairman Hans Blix, however, contended that Iraq had not provided a complete declaration of its weapons program.

They alleged, for example, that Iraq sought to acquire uranium in Africa that could be used to make nuclear weapons. The evidence for this claim, however, was judged by the CIA to be doubtful even at the time Bush and Blair made the charge; later it was conclusively proved to be a forgery.

The Return of UN Weapons Inspectors to Iraq

After much behind-the-scenes negotiating, the United States and Britain succeeded in getting Resolution 1441 adopted by a unanimous vote of the UN Security Council on November 8, 2002. The resolution provided Iraq "a final opportunity to comply with [UN] disarmament obligations"[26] and set up a new inspections process. The resolution called on Iraq to provide immediate, unimpeded, unconditional, and unrestricted access to weapons inspectors. In addition, the resolution gave Iraq thirty days to provide the UN with an accurate and complete declaration of all aspects of its programs to develop chemical, biological, and nuclear weapons, ballistic missiles, and other delivery systems. Finally, the resolution warned Iraq that it would "face serious consequences as a result of its continued violations of its obligations."[27] Iraq agreed to allow weapons inspectors back into Iraq, and inspections by the International Atomic Energy Agency (IAEA) and the newly formed UN weapons inspection team, called the UN Monitoring, Verification and Inspection Commission (UNMOVIC), began in late November 2002.

In January 2003 UNMOVIC and IAEA reported to the UN that they had received free access to Iraqi facilities and had been able to conduct more than 350 on-site inspections but that no weapons of mass destruction had been discovered. UNMOVIC chairman Dr. Hans Blix, for example, told the Security Council on January 9, 2003, "If we had found any 'smoking gun' we would have reported it to the Council. . . . We have not submitted any such reports."[28] IAEA director general Dr. Mohamed El Baradei similarly reported that no evidence of nuclear activities had been detected.

Blix, however, told the UN that Iraq had not provided a full and complete declaration of its weapons programs as required by Resolution 1441. Although twelve thousand pages in length, Blix said the Iraqi weapons declaration of December 7, 2002, was practically devoid of new evidence and failed to resolve many of the unanswered questions about Iraqi weapons capabilities that remained from the earlier UN weapons inspection process (1991 to 1998). Subsequent reports by Blix in February and March similarly reported that inspectors found no prohibited weapons of mass destruction and that Iraq was offering only limited cooperation.

The United States Says Iraq Not Cooperating

Despite the lack of a "smoking gun" showing Iraq in possession of weapons of mass destruction, the United States believed after several months of inspections that Saddam Hussein, by failing to cooperate and hiding evidence, had demonstrated that he had no intention of disarming and every intention of continuing to obstruct the UN. On February 5, 2003, in an attempt to convince the world to act against Iraq, U.S. secretary of state Colin Powell spoke at the UN:

> Iraq's behavior demonstrate[s] that Saddam Hussein and his regime have made no effort—no effort—to disarm as required by the international community. Indeed, the facts and Iraq's behavior show that Saddam Hussein and his regime are concealing their efforts to produce more weapons of mass destruction.[29]

In his speech Powell revealed a seemingly impressive list of U.S. intelligence information, including not only information obtained from Iraqi defectors but also audio tapes of cell phone conversations between Iraqi military officers (purportedly discussing how to hide evidence from inspectors) and satellite photos (showing that Iraq had recently moved banned weapons materials from a number of Iraqi weapons of mass destruction facilities). Powell also claimed U.S. intelligence showed that Iraq had mobile laboratories used to make biological weapons and conceal these activities from the UN.

In addition, Powell cited Iraq's refusal to allow Iraqi scientists who might know about weapons of mass destruction to be interviewed by the UN without an Iraqi military representative present. Iraq's insistence on monitoring its scientists, together with direct threats by Hussein against scientists who revealed sensitive information, said Powell, intimidated the scientists and crippled the UN's best source of information about Iraqi weapons programs. Finally, Powell argued there was a direct link

Colin Powell holds up a vial that he described as one that could contain anthrax during a presentation to the UN Security Council.

Some European leaders, including French foreign minister Dominique de Villepin (left), French president Jaques Chirac (center, right), and German foreign minister Joschka Fischer (center, left), opposed a war with Iraq.

between Saddam Hussein and terrorism, referring to the al-Zarqawi evidence previously cited by the administration:

> The . . . nexus between Iraq and the Al Qaida terrorist network, a nexus that combines classic terrorist organizations and modern methods of murder. Iraq today harbors a deadly terrorist network headed by Abu Musab Al-Zarqawi, an associate and collaborator of Osama bin Laden and his Al Qaida lieutenants.[30]

Powell also claimed that Iraqi officials had met with al-Qaeda terrorists on several occasions since the early 1990s.

After Powell's speech, however, much of Powell's intelligence information was challenged as less than persuasive. Indeed, even some administration and CIA officials admitted that the United States did not know what prohibited materials the audio tapes might be referring to and that the evidence on al-Zarqawi did not clearly establish that Iraq was harboring al-Qaeda terrorists.

Nevertheless, on February 24 the United States, Britain, and Spain circulated a second UN resolution to authorize war against Iraq; the proposed resolution concluded that "Iraq has failed to take the final opportunity afforded to it [by] resolution 1441 (2002)."[31]

UN Opposition to Military Action Against Iraq

Despite the strong push by the United States and Britain, however, key members of the UN Security Council, particularly France, Germany, and Russia, refused to authorize military action against Iraq. They believed that continued inspections provided the best way to contain Saddam Hussein's threat. French foreign minister Dominique de Villepin, for example, argued that "since we can disarm Iraq through peaceful means, we should not take the risk to endanger the lives of innocent civilians or soldiers, to jeopardize the stability of the region, and further widen the gap between our people and our cultures."[32] These opponents of U.S. action also feared that war in Iraq might fuel more terrorism. For example, German foreign minister Joschka Fischer warned that a military strike against Iraq "would involve considerable and unpredictable risks for the global fight against terrorism."[33]

Citing the fact that no weapons of mass destruction had been found, these countries circulated a memo at the UN in February 2003 urging that war must be a last resort. The memo proposed that "reinforced inspections, a clear timeline and the military build-up provide[d] a realistic means . . . to exert maximum pressure on Iraq."[34] In March, China joined the demand for more time for inspections. As weeks passed, it became increasingly clear that the United States could not muster the nine out of fifteen Security Council votes it needed

to pass a second resolution; even if the United States did get enough votes, a veto by permanent council members France or Russia looked entirely possible.

"Coalition of the Willing"

When the United States was unable to secure the needed support for a second UN resolution authorizing military action, U.S. president Bush moved forward with U.S. plans to invade Iraq and remove Saddam Hussein from power, as the leader of a group of nations that he called a "coalition of the willing."

In a speech to the nation on March 17, 2003, Bush announced U.S. war plans:

> Today, no nation can possibly claim that Iraq has disarmed, and it will not disarm so long as Saddam Hussein holds power. . . . All the decades of deceit and cruelty have now reached an end. Saddam Hussein and his sons must leave Iraq within 48 hours. Their refusal to do so will result in military conflict, commenced at a time of our choosing.[35]

Saddam Hussein, however, did not leave Iraq as demanded by the United States, and so began the march toward war. On March 18, 2003, UNMOVIC and IAEA inspectors withdrew from Iraq after the UN secretary-general announced his decision to withdraw all UN staff. That same day U.S. secretary of state Colin Powell announced that the "coalition of the willing" included some thirty nations. However, only Britain and Australia provided any

Cars transporting UN weapons inspectors head for Baghdad's airport. Under the threat of war, weapons inspectors withdrew from Iraq on March 18, 2003.

significant military assistance. The other coalition countries included Afghanistan, Albania, Azerbaijan, Bulgaria, Colombia, the Czech Republic, Denmark, El Salvador, Eritrea, Estonia, Ethiopia, Georgia, Hungary, Italy, Japan, South Korea, Latvia, Lithuania, Macedonia, the Netherlands, Nicaragua, the Philippines, Poland, Romania, Slovakia, Spain, Turkey, and Uzbekistan.

Notably, unlike the coalition that supported the first Gulf War, this list of supporting countries did not include traditional European allies except for Britain or any Arab nations. This lack of allied or UN support for the action and America's decision to essentially "go it alone" created a precedent many countries believed was dangerous for future global relations. If powerful nations like the United States could act against the will of the international community, many argued, the value of international bodies such as the UN could be diminished and the U.S. actions could be viewed as illegitimate.

Chapter Three

Shock and Awe in Twenty-Six Days

As the United States prepared for military action against Iraq, U.S. officials confidently named the U.S. battle plan "Shock and Awe" for the psychological impact that its overwhelming force would have on Iraqis. Vice President Dick Cheney predicted that the United States would easily win victory and that U.S. troops would be greeted as liberators. These positive forecasts, however, met with a much different reality, as U.S. troops encountered early fierce resistance from the enemy and as crowds of thankful Iraqis failed to materialize for U.S. and international television cameras. The real shock and awe for Iraqis, however, occurred a few weeks later when U.S. troops regained momentum and easily took the capital city of Baghdad, leading to the sudden collapse of the Saddam Hussein regime after decades of repression and terror.

Initial Strike on Saddam Hussein

The U.S. Pentagon's Shock and Awe campaign was supposed to begin with warplanes and ships launching between three and four hundred cruise missiles into Iraq on the first day, more than the total number of missiles launched during the whole of the first Gulf War in 1991, followed by a similar assault the following day. In a surprise move, however, on the evening of March 19, 2003, President Bush instead ordered a limited missile strike on a specific target in Baghdad believed to be the command post for Saddam Hussein and top leaders of his regime. The United States hoped to kill Saddam Hussein in one decisive blow and thereby decapitate his twenty-four-year-old dictatorship.

A warship launches a missile toward Iraq. The war began with a surprise missile strike against what the United States believed was Saddam Hussein's command post.

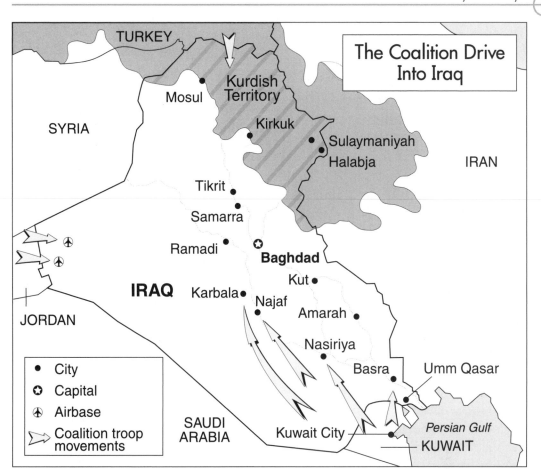

The Coalition Drive Into Iraq

The attack was launched using cruise missiles from ships in the Red Sea and the Persian Gulf followed by bombs dropped by U.S. F-117 Nighthawk stealth fighter jets. Later, U.S. secretary of defense Donald H. Rumsfeld explained that the strike was carried out on the basis of very good intelligence information and confirmed that the target was a senior Iraqi leadership compound. Iraq responded to the missile attack by firing missiles at allied troops in Kuwait; many of those missed and others were intercepted before striking their targets.

A few hours after the attack, however, Saddam Hussein appeared in a videotape on Iraqi television, raising the possibility that he had survived and that the U.S. mission had failed. Analysts later concluded that the voice on the videotape was Hussein's but said it could have been recorded earlier. Moreover, military analysts said that although the Iraqi command bunkers were severely damaged and there was a dramatic drop in communication from the command post, there was no confirmation that Hussein and his aides had been killed.

The Air and Ground War Begins

In addition to the attack on Saddam Hussein, the U.S. military began to set the stage for the planned all-out air and land assault on Iraq, a plan the military called Operation Iraqi Freedom. The United States and its allies positioned ground troops to the south of Iraq along the Kuwait-Iraq border, and on March 19 allied warplanes attacked Iraqi artillery pieces in this southern area because they posed a threat to U.S. and British troops stationed there. Also, the United States began a psychological operations campaign that issued instructions to Iraqi troops on how to surrender to allied forces once the war began. The messages were delivered by a radio station near the Kuwaiti-Iraqi border operated by American Special Operations forces, by an airborne radio station, and by leaflets dropped by allied aircraft. Iraqis were instructed to park their vehicles, put white flags on them, move more than half a mile away from their vehicles, and wait for further instructions.

On March 21, 2003, the long-awaited Shock and Awe military campaign against Iraq began. The first round of air strikes dropped more than thirteen hundred cruise missiles and bombs on command and control targets in Baghdad. The strikes were intended to destroy Saddam Hussein's ability to communicate with and control his forces. Targets included headquarters and facilities used by Hussein's special armed forces, including the Republican Guard,

Hussein's most elite troops, and the Special Republican Guard, an even more elite group in charge of protecting Hussein and thwarting any coup attempts. The air assault continued unabated in the following days, pounding Baghdad day and night, taking out government facilities, destroying Iraq's air defenses, and hitting Republican Guard positions that guarded the city.

Also on March 21, U.S. Marine and Army and British ground forces numbering about 150,000 began a long march toward Baghdad as part of a southern front. The land assault originally had been planned to occur days later, after air strikes and special operations had prepared Iraq for invasion. In order to retain the element of surprise, however, the attack was moved up after the early strike on Saddam Hussein. In addition, Iraq had started fires in six oil fields in southern Iraq, and the United States was anxious to protect Iraqi oil.

The campaign got off to a highly successful start, raising high expectations among the U.S. public that the war could be won easily and painlessly. Coalition ground forces advanced quickly through the weakly defended southern desert of Iraq; within the first day, troops raced to within 200 miles of Baghdad. Television images showed American bombs striking targets in Baghdad with great precision and American tanks gliding swiftly across the Iraqi deserts.

Unexpected Iraqi Resistance

As the war in Iraq unfolded, contrary to American predictions, Iraqis fighting for the Hussein regime appeared to be neither

U.S. Marines advance toward Baghdad. Soldiers met with fierce resistance as they fought their way to the capital.

shocked nor awed by the American military campaign. Although the first days of fighting appeared successful for the United States and precision air strikes accurately pounded military targets in Baghdad and elsewhere, coalition ground forces quickly met fierce resistance from Iraqi fighters.

The first setbacks came over the weekend of March 23, near the Iraqi cities of Basra and Nasiriya in southern Iraq, and at the seaside port of Umm Qasr, near Kuwait. Coalition forces surrounded these areas to allow the main force of allied troops to con-tinue to proceed toward Baghdad. However, firefights broke out as Iraqi troops attacked the U.S. and British forces at those locations. Also, the column of tanks headed for Baghdad was repeatedly attacked by small bands of Iraqi guerrilla fighters, who were heavily armed and who sought to harass the allied forces' progress. These fighters, known as the Saddam Fedayeen, or "Martyrs of Saddam," were not part of the regular Iraqi army but were special forces loyal to Saddam Hussein trained in terror-ist and guerrilla tactics.

In addition, coalition forces began to suffer casualties. An army maintenance company was captured after it took a wrong turn and became separated from the Third Infantry Division near Nasiriya. Twelve American soldiers were reported missing. Five of the twelve, one of them a woman, were shown on the Arabic television station, Al Jazeera, looking scared and angry. At the end of the day on March 23, U.S. mil-

Saving Private Jessica Lynch

As U.S. troops gained confidence in the drive to Baghdad, other events also helped bolster American morale. On April 2, in a much-publicized story, U.S. special operations forces rescued army private Jessica Lynch from the Saddam Hospital in Nasiriya, Iraq, where she had been held captive since March 23. Lynch, a nineteen-year-old from Palestine, West Virginia, was one of fifteen members of the 507th Ordinance Maintenance Company, which was attacked by Iraqi forces early in the war. Her rescue became possible after an Iraqi citizen bravely reported her location to the U.S. military.

Later, Lynch's rescue became controversial in the United States as evidence surfaced suggesting that it might have been staged by the United States to create positive publicity for the U.S. war effort among Americans at home. Interviews of Iraqi doctors in the Iraqi hospital where Lynch was being treated claimed that the U.S. rescue was greatly overdramatized. For example, they said that U.S. commandos refused a key and instead broke down doors and entered with their guns drawn. They used helicopter and armored vehicle backup even though there was no Iraqi military presence and no resistance from the hospital staff. Indeed, some said the raid by the U.S. military was unnecessary because they were trying to turn Lynch over to U.S. authorities. U.S. military officials, however, defended the action, arguing that troops did not know Iraqis wanted to hand over Lynch, or what they might encounter at the hospital, and that American military doctrine calls for using overwhelming force in such situations.

Jessica Lynch is transported to a military hospital after being rescued on April 2, 2003.

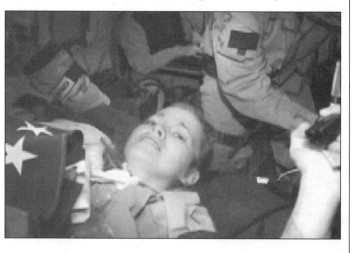

itary officials reported a total of at least twenty American soldiers missing or killed and up to eighty-two wounded.

The March to Baghdad

Thereafter, resistance continued as allied troops moved closer to Baghdad. Fighting continued in southern Iraq, and in a major setback for the Americans, Iraqis successfully attacked a large group of American Apache helicopters. A group of about thirty Apache helicopters was hit with a hail of antiaircraft fire and rocket-launched grenades while on a night combat mission targeting units of the Republican Guard. Two of the Apache helicopters were forced down, and two American crew members were later captured by the Iraqis. The remaining thirty Apaches were forced to return to base, almost all of them damaged.

A bitter fight was also fought around Najaf, a city about ninety miles from Baghdad and an Islamic holy site, considerably slowing the U.S. Army's march northward. Again the Iraqi forces fighting in Najaf appeared to be not regular army, but mostly militia fighters from Hussein's Baath Party and two other groups, Saddam Fedayeen and Al Quds.

On top of these troubles the U.S. march to Baghdad was slowed by the weather and hindered by a lack of Iraqi assistance. A huge sandstorm disrupted the American convoys, blinded night-vision goggles, and damaged equipment including guns, helicopters, and computers. Moreover, contrary to U.S. hopes, Shia Muslims in southern

Iraqi cities did not rise up against Saddam Hussein, oppose the guerrilla attacks on Americans, or greet coalition troops as liberators.

Finally, on March 24 Saddam Hussein appeared on Iraqi television to defiantly urge Iraqis to fight coalition invaders. "Strike them until they come to the conclusion that they are not in a position to commit crimes against you and your people," said Hussein. "God has ordered you to cut their throats."[36] Hussein also demonstrated that he was aware of recent military events, mentioning for example that soldiers of Iraq's Eleventh Brigade had waged a heroic battle at Umm Qasr and praising individual Iraqi commanders fighting in southern Iraq. Hussein's message was clearly recorded earlier, but it clarified for most observers that he had survived the earlier U.S. missile strike.

In the United States, the events of the first weeks of the war caused many to criticize the U.S. war plan. The *New York Times*, for example, in an editorial charged that the U.S. ground force was too small, questioning "the American decision to press ahead with a relatively small invasion force supported by overwhelming air and missile power."[37] This war plan, the newspaper said, created a lack of security for American troops as well as Iraqi civilians.

Indeed, even Lieutenant General William Wallace, the commander of U.S. Army forces in the gulf, admitted the small bands of guerrillas were a challenge to American troops. "The enemy we're fighting is a bit different than the one we war-gamed against, because of these para-military forces," he said. "We knew they were here, but we did not know how they would fight."[38] As a result of the unexpected Iraqi resistance and the limited ground forces, the U.S. military planners were forced to adapt: They delayed the battle of Baghdad and focused their efforts on rooting out the pro-Hussein guerrilla groups in southern and central Iraqi cities.

The early events in Iraq also caused President Bush to try to prepare the American people for a longer war than they had initially expected. Speaking on the White House lawn on March 24, Bush said, "It is evident that it's going to take a while to achieve our objective." He added, "I can assure the American people we're making good progress, and I can also assure them that this is just the beginning of a tough fight."[39]

The Fall of Baghdad

Despite the setbacks, however, U.S. and British troops celebrated a number of successes during the first two weeks of the war

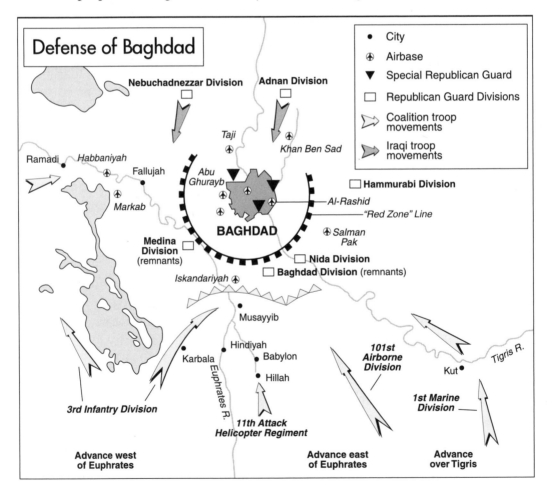

Defense of Baghdad

- • City
- ⊕ Airbase
- ▼ Special Republican Guard
- ☐ Republican Guard Divisions
- ⇒ Coalition troop movements
- ⇒ Iraqi troop movements

Nebuchadnezzar Division
Adnan Division
Taji
Khan Ben Sad
Ramadi
Habbaniyah
Fallujah
Abu Ghurayb
☐ Hammurabi Division
Markab
Al-Rashid
"Red Zone" Line
BAGHDAD
Medina Division (remnants)
⊕ Salman Pak
Iskandariyah
☐ Nida Division
☐ Baghdad Division (remnants)
Musayyib
Hindiyah
Babylon
101st Airborne Division
Kut
Tigris R.
Karbala
Euphrates R.
Hillah
1st Marine Division
3rd Infantry Division
11th Attack Helicopter Regiment

Advance west of Euphrates
Advance east of Euphrates
Advance over Tigris

American tanks roll into Baghdad. Despite some heavy fighting, allied forces arrived in Iraq's capital less than one month after the war began.

and made steady progress toward the ultimate goal of attacking Baghdad. Iraqi oil fields, for example, were quickly secured, preventing any widespread sabotage by Iraqi loyalists. In addition, although Iraq was able to launch missiles into Kuwait, the U.S. antimissile system shot down most of them, preventing any damage to Kuwait or U.S. command centers there. Most important, American forces had traveled deep into Iraq to the outskirts of Baghdad. The next phase of the campaign required U.S. troops to defeat the Republican Guard divisions that Saddam Hussein had positioned to defend the Iraqi capital and then to begin ground attacks against Baghdad itself.

By April 2, U.S. Army and Marine ground troops had entered an area that military planners called the "red zone," a circle about fifty miles outside of Baghdad that was within artillery and missile range of Republican Guard forces defending Baghdad. Thereafter, one by one, U.S. forces easily destroyed Republican Guard units such as the Medina Division, the Baghdad Division, and the Nida Division, which were expected to put up a much tougher fight. Also, to aid in the Baghdad assault, the American military captured Baghdad's international airport for use in refueling allied warplanes. By April 4, U.S. forces had advanced to the Baghdad city limits.

The following day, in a surprise move, a group of sixty American tanks and other vehicles rolled into Baghdad, killing thousands of Iraqi fighters. The U.S. military said it wanted to send a message to Iraq that it was in control: "We just wanted to let them know that we're here,"[40] said Major General Buford C. Blount III, commander of the U.S. Army's Third Infantry Division. In addition, allied forces may have wanted to respond to an appearance by Saddam Hussein on the streets of Baghdad the day before. Iraqi television had shown Hussein smiling amongst a cheering crowd of supporters, proving that he had survived despite all U.S. attempts to destroy him.

Over the next few days American and British forces made progressively bolder moves into the city, occupying major presidential palaces and establishing a permanent presence there. With the success in Baghdad the momentum of the war seemed

A U.S. tank helps Iraqi citizens topple a statue of Saddam Hussein on April 9, 2003. Many Iraqis cheered as the statue crashed to the ground.

to change, leading supporters of President Bush to claim victory. Vice President Dick Cheney, for example, said the U.S. advance into Baghdad was proof that early criticism of the war plan was wrong; instead, he said, the war was "one of the most extraordinary military campaigns ever conducted."[41]

The Collapse of Saddam Hussein's Regime

On April 9 the world witnessed the most striking image of the war: In the center of Baghdad, in a scene reminiscent of the fall of the Berlin Wall in 1989 (the wall that had separated East and West Germany since the end of World War II), Iraqi citizens with help from U.S. Marines toppled a towering bronze statue of Saddam Hussein. As the statue came crashing to the ground, a crowd of jubilant Iraqis cheered loudly, danced for joy, and hit the statue with their shoes, a gesture of contempt in Iraq. At this moment, psychologically at least, the regime of Saddam Hussein collapsed. Brigadeer General Vincent K. Brooks summarized the victory at a briefing at U.S. command headquarters, stating, "Today the regime is in disarray. The capital city has been added to those places where the regime has lost control."[42]

The scene in Baghdad signaled that the war would soon be over. American officials, however, cautioned that much remained to be done before victory could be declared. As U.S. and British forces continued to consolidate their hold on Baghdad, the U.S. focus shifted to northern Iraq. Soon Kurdish fighters there, under the command of American special forces, took control of the oil town of Kirkuk, followed by efforts to stabilize the northern city of Mosul after Iraqi troops stationed there withdrew.

Finally, U.S. troops made an assault on Tikrit, Saddam Hussein's hometown, considered to be the last holdout for remnants of forces loyal to his regime. Tikrit was expected to pose a significant obstacle to coalition forces, but instead it was taken on April 14 with little opposition. Finally, on April 15, 2003, military officials at the U.S. Pentagon said the main fighting in Iraq was finished, and President Bush declared that "the regime of Saddam Hussein is no more."[43]

Finding Saddam and Baath Officials

It was clear, unfortunately, that Saddam Hussein had likely survived the attack on his country. U.S. forces, however, had no idea where Hussein was hiding. Rumors abounded, suggesting that he had fled to Syria, that he was hiding in Tikrit, or that he was still in Baghdad. Wherever he and his supporters were, the United States badly wanted to find and destroy them, to ease the minds of still-frightened Iraqis who had lived under his brutal regime for decades and to ensure that he could not make an effort to return to power.

The U.S. military, therefore, acting on tips and intelligence information, made additional attempts to attack locations where Hussein and other members of the Iraqi leadership were believed to be meeting. On April 7, for example, American

Recovering from Saddam's Evils

The end of the war and the removal of Saddam Hussein from power reminded Iraqis of the horrible terror of Hussein's regime and the many gruesome ways that the regime punished those accused of political crimes or threats against the government. As American soldiers gained control of Iraqi prisons and palaces, for example, they uncovered clear evidence of the regime's brutality, including torture equipment used to deliver electric shocks to ears and genitals and cages used to hold human prisoners. Evidence of this brutality also was revealed in the numbers of Iraqi citizens who have been mutilated by surgeons on Hussein's orders; the cutting off of ears appears to have been a favorite punishment. In addition, thousands of Iraqi families whose relatives were arrested or disappeared during Hussein's rule began learning for the first time about the fates of their family members. The bodies of these political prisoners were discovered in graveyards throughout Iraq, largely because the Hussein government kept highly accurate records of people it killed.

It may take a long time for Iraqis to recover psychologically from twenty-four years of terror. Reporters Melinda Liu, Rod Nordland, and Evan Thomas explained in an April 2003 *Newsweek* article entitled "The Saddam Files":

> America wants to bring liberty and democracy to Iraq. But first the Iraqis will have to come to terms with the legacy of fear Saddam created, and regain the humanity that was frightened and beaten out of them by three decades of grotesque misrule.

The turning point for Iraqis may be the killing or capture of Saddam Hussein; many Iraqis fear that as long as Saddam Hussein remains uncaptured, he may at some time in the future try to regain power in Iraq.

Iraqis walk among plastic bags containing bodies exhumed from a mass grave south of Baghdad.

bombers dropped four bunker-busting two-thousand-pound bombs on a compound in the Mansur area of Baghdad, where military officials believed Hussein was meeting with his sons and top leaders. The bomb created a huge crater sixty feet deep and killed as many as fourteen Iraqis. Afterward U.S. officials said they were not sure whether Hussein survived, but troops did not secure the site, suggesting to some that Hussein had not been hit.

Later that week, on April 10, American forces attacked and later bombed a mosque in Baghdad where Hussein was reported to have been seen. Some claimed that Hussein or one of his aides had been hit in the earlier bombing and had been taken to the mosque, suffering from wounds. Neighbors claimed Hussein had visited the mosque the day before: "Saddam was here, and I kissed him," one man said, "People were kissing his feet. They were cheering. There were 200 people there."[44] However, by the time marines attacked, members of Hussein's group had already escaped.

In an effort to encourage the capture of Hussein and his top aides, the U.S. military in April announced rewards and issued troops a deck of fifty-five playing cards showing pictures and names of the most-wanted Iraqi leaders. On April 17 troops captured Barzan Ibrahim Hasan al-Tikriti, Hussein's half-brother and a former chief of Iraqi intelligence, who is believed to have helped Hussein hide billions of dollars in other countries. A few days later, Hussein's son-in-law Jamal Mustafa Abdallah Sultan surrendered; he

served as deputy head of tribal affairs and was involved in the special security organization headed by Saddam's son Qusay. As time passed, others were taken into custody, including Tariq Aziz, Iraq's deputy prime minister and public spokesman for the regime; General Abid Hamid Mahmoud al-Tikriti, Hussein's top aide; and many other high-level government officials and prominent scientists.

Much later, U.S. troops acting on a tip from an Iraqi even located and killed Saddam's two sons, Qusay and Odai.

Saddam Hussein, however, remained unaccounted for. Finally, on April 30 a London-based Arabic newspaper, *Al Quds al Arabi*, printed an ominous handwritten letter said to be written and signed by Saddam Hussein. The letter urged Iraqis to rebel against the "infidel, criminal, murderous and cowardly occupier," promised that those who collaborated with the Americans would be punished, and predicted that "the day of liberation and victory will come."[45] The letter was dated April 28, Hussein's sixty-sixth birthday. It confirmed many Iraqis' worst fears—that Hussein was still hiding in Iraq and waiting to stage a comeback.

The Search for Weapons of Mass Destruction

Throughout the war, coalition military planners and troops were fearful that Iraq would use chemical weapons against them. These fears, however, were never realized. Although American soldiers approaching Baghdad repeatedly found indicators of

U.S. weapons experts search for chemical weapons near the city of Basra. As the war ended, the military focused on uncovering Saddam Hussein's suspected cache of chemical, biological, and nuclear weapons.

chemical weapons, such as gas masks, protective suits, nerve gas antidotes, training manuals, and barrels of suspicious chemicals, chemical weapons were never used by Iraqi troops. As the war ended, the focus of the military turned to searching for Iraq's supposedly hidden cache of weapons of mass destruction. This goal became a high priority for the United States, because find-ing and destroying illegal weapons was the main justification given by President Bush in his push for war against Iraq.

Despite expectations that troops would quickly stumble upon illegal weapons left behind by Iraqi forces, however, initial coalition efforts to search for such weapons proved unsuccessful. On April 20 news reports suggested a possible explanation for why neither UN weapons inspectors nor U.S. forces had yet found any weapons of mass destruction. A scientist who claimed to have worked in Iraq's chemical weapons program told an American military team hunting illegal weapons that Iraq had destroyed chemical weapons and biological warfare equipment a few days before the war began. The scientist led U.S. troops to buried material used as the building block for a toxic agent used in illegal chemical weapons.

In addition, the scientist, whose identity was kept secret by the military, claimed that, beginning in the mid-1990s, Iraq had destroyed some stockpiles of unconventional weapons, sent some to Syria, and recently had burned some warehouses of chemical agents. Hussein had supposedly focused on projects that would be almost impossible for weapons inspectors to detect—for example, hiding chemical ingredients that were not prohibited as weapons but that could be quickly made into chemical weapons.

As weeks passed, American military units found parts of three mobile labs that they claimed might be mobile biological weapons laboratories. The labs appeared to have been cleaned by the Iraqis, and U.S. experts who tested the labs reported on May 19 that they had failed to find biological agents. Nevertheless, these experts concluded that the only plausible use for the units was to produce germs for weapons, a finding that bolstered U.S. prewar assertions that such mobile labs were being used by the Iraqis to hide illicit biological and chemical weapons. This U.S. conclusion about the labs, however, was challenged by other U.S. and British intelligence experts. Meanwhile, U.S. teams continued to search a list of more than one thousand sites that American officials have identified as possible hiding spots for weapons.

As a result of the lack of success in finding prohibited weapons, President Bush came under growing international pressure. An editorial in the *New York Times*, for example, said, "with every passing day, American credibility is called into question. ... The chief justification for invading Iraq was to get rid of Baghdad's stores of chemical and biological agents and dismantle its effort to produce a nuclear bomb."[46] Also, the CIA was ordered to begin a review to determine whether it may have erred in its prewar assessments of Iraq's weapons programs. Otherwise, President Bush steadfastly insisted that the United States would find the hidden weapons, cautioning that it would just take time.

The War's Message to the World

The U.S. war in Iraq was the first action taken under a new national security strategy created by President Bush, called "preemption." This policy calls for the United States to intervene before a potential enemy can attack America. As President Bush explained in a radio address in early April, his decision to attack Iraq was part of his plan to "not sit and wait, leaving enemies free to plot another September 11—this time, perhaps, with chemical, biological or nuclear terror."[47]

The war thus demonstrated to the rest of the world that America is capable and willing to take action to change a regime that poses a potential future threat to U.S. interests. This message was not lost on other countries, such North Korea, Iran, and Syria, which were also believed to be developing weapons of mass destruction and have connections to terrorists. Although the Bush administration insisted that it had no plans to conduct other preventative wars against countries such as these, U.S. officials hoped the threat of U.S. action would cause other rogue nations to modify their behavior.

North Korea, for example, appeared to change its bargaining posture after the U.S. action in Iraq. After insisting for months that it would only negotiate with the United States about its nuclear weapons program, North Korean negotiators agreed to multicountry talks with both China and the United States in late April 2003. However, at the talks North Korea announced that it had already developed nuclear weapons and might even choose to sell them to other countries. North Korea's threat, for many, showed the other possible outcome of the example of the Iraq war—that small countries, instead of halting weapons development out of fear, might instead speed up their nuclear weapons development to deter possible U.S. strikes similar to the one against Iraq.

South Korean and North Korean leaders discuss North Korea's nuclear program in 2003. North Korea announced that it had developed nuclear weapons and might sell them to other countries.

Indeed, critics of the war in Iraq claim that the war will not make the United States or the world safer but instead will increase the spread of nuclear weapons and inspire more terrorism. The failure of the United States to secure nuclear waste sites in Iraq led to looting of nuclear materials, and experts warn that, because of the war, this nuclear material might end up more quickly in the hands of terrorists, creating an even more dangerous terrorist threat. Also, the images of the U.S. invasion of an Arab country, critics say, are bound to inspire more anti-American terrorist attacks. This prediction appeared to come true quickly—in May 2003, suicide bombers believed to be connected to al-Qaeda hit American targets in Saudi Arabia.

At the very least the war appears to have created more, not less, animosity toward America. A June 2003 report by the nonpartisan Pew Research Center for the People and the Press, according to its director, Andrew Kohut, found that

> the war has widened the rift between Americans and Western Europeans, further inflamed the Muslim world, softened support for the war on terrorism, and significantly weakened global public support for the pillars of the post–World War II era—the U.N. and the North Atlantic alliance.[48]

Whether these seemingly negative interpretations of the war will be recorded by history as the war's legacy, however, may depend at least partly on the success of postwar nation-building and peacemaking efforts.

Chapter Four

The Aftermath of War in Iraq

The Bush administration claimed that the war was a great military victory for America because it resulted in the quick removal of Saddam Hussein's regime and freedom for the Iraqi people. For Iraq, however, the reality of the war's aftermath was death and destruction, a power vacuum, and chaos in the streets. Thousands of Iraqis were killed or injured by American bombs, and the cutoff of essential services such as water, food, and electricity created humanitarian disasters in the making. Without a police force to maintain order, looting and crime became widespread, depriving communities of many items essential for recovery and rebuilding. Slowly the United States began to restore order, restart essential services, and lay the groundwork for creation of an interim Iraqi government. America, however, appeared much less prepared for postwar challenges than it was for war.

Civilian Deaths and Injuries

Much was made throughout the war of the precision of America's bombs and their ability to strike military targets in Baghdad and other areas without causing "collateral damage," the military's term for civilian deaths. American forces also took great care in selecting targets to limit civilian casualties. In addition, U.S. military officials touted the low casualty rate for U.S. and British soldiers—a total of 162 were killed during the war.

However, either because hard numbers were unavailable or because they wanted to downplay the information, U.S. reports did not mention that unknown thousands of Iraqi troops were killed and wounded, many of them forced to fight against their will. As for civilians, reports varied but a survey by the *Associated Press*, based on records from 60 of Iraq's 124 hospitals and reported in June 2003, said that "at least 3,240 civilians died . . . between March 20, when the war began, and April 20, when the fighting was dying down."[49] Thousands more were injured by the attacks.

These civilian casualties, though perhaps low in number given the amount of firepower directed at Iraq, rival the numbers killed and wounded in the September 11 attack on the United States and represent untold suffering for many families across Iraq. These casualties also were the main focus of sensational Arab television

Iraqis carry the body of a man killed by a U.S. air strike. Despite the great care American forces took to limit strikes to military targets, many civilians were killed or injured during the war.

reporting throughout the war, stirring Arab anger at the American invasion of an Arab country.

Humanitarian Concerns— Water and Food

As the war raged, it disrupted supplies of water, food, and electricity, raising fears of humanitarian disasters. Indeed, even before the war Iraqis were already suffering from Iraq's previous wars and twelve years of UN-imposed economic sanctions. These events destroyed Iraq's middle class and produced deaths, chronic malnutrition, and disease among Iraq's population. For example, at the time the war started, Iraqis barely had enough food; as the British periodical the *Economist* notes, "Before the first bomb was dropped, 16m [million] people—six Iraqis in ten—depended entirely on the OFFP [the UN's oil-for-food program] for food."[50] Iraq's

U.S. soldiers hand out food to Iraqi citizens. Food shortages in Iraq before and during the war were widespread and led to chronic malnutrition and disease.

water supply also was already contaminated from the leakage of sewage into fresh water supplies. Another war only made things worse.

Among the first concerns was restoring an adequate water supply. When the fighting knocked out electrical power for water treatment plants, people's only source of safe drinking water was destroyed, leaving them to drink water from sources that may have been contaminated by sewage or other sources. In Basra the problem became acute quickly. As soon as British troops were able to gain control of the city, they began to ship in clean water. However, this was not enough, and by May 12 the World Health Organization began warning that Basra might experience an epidemic of cholera, a disease caused by germs from fecal contamination of water supplies that results in severe diarrhea and sometimes death from dehydration. The International Committee of the Red Cross (ICRC) managed to restore water to half the population in Basra, but many continued to rely on water from polluted estuaries.

Food became the next essential to prevent humanitarian crises in Iraq. The UN oil-for-food program was suspended on March 17, just before the war began, although extra food was distributed before that time to allow people to stock up. The UN at that time estimated, however, that food supplies would soon run out. The UN's World Food Programme (WFP), fortunately, positioned enough food in nearby areas to feed 2 million people for one month, but after that it expected to face an unprecedented challenge to feed Iraq's population. On March 28 the WFP appealed to donors to provide $2.2 billion in food aid for Iraq, the amount it estimated would be necessary to cover humanitarian assistance for Iraq for a mere six months.

Fortunately, the world began responding to the need for humanitarian aid in Iraq. On March 28, for example, the British delivered emergency food, blankets, and medicine to the port of Umm Qasr after the waterway was cleared of mines, and shortly thereafter the WFP was able to truck supplies of dry milk into northern Iraq. Also in March the UN temporarily resumed distribution of OFFP food but voted to phase out the oil-for-food program after six months. When the war ended, the OFFP had assets of about $13 billion, but much of it was earmarked to pay contracts for food, medicine, and industrial goods that had been approved earlier. By early April, according to the *Economist*, "about $10 billion worth of supplies [were] in the pipeline, and the UN [had] designated more than 450 contracts for medicines, health supplies, food, water and sanitation, worth over $1 billion, as priorities for shipment."[51] Countries also began donating aid. The United States was the largest contributor: On March 25, President Bush asked Congress for $2.4 billion for relief and reconstruction, bringing the U.S. total contribution to $3.5 billion at that time.

Iraqis, however, remain concerned about the long-term food situation. For example, Iraq relies on an area called Mosul to produce half of its wheat and barley, but

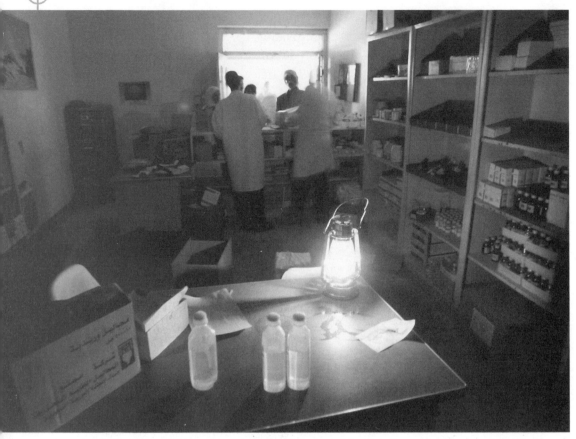

Iraqi medical personnel work in a dark hospital during a blackout. Even after the war ended, power outages remained a problem in areas outside Baghdad.

the harvest there is in serious jeopardy. Under Hussein's rule, the government would set a price for the grain and pay the farmers; Iraq had no government, its banks had been looted, fuel was in short supply, and land disputes were increasing, creating formidable difficulties for farmers and threatening Iraq's food supply.

Electrical power was restored by late April to many parts of Baghdad, but other parts were left without power or were experiencing frequent blackouts. Officials predicted that the power shortage would last well into the summer of 2003. Authorities established priorities for who would get power: Hospitals were first, then water treatment plants, sewage treatment plants, and homes, with industry last on the list.

Health Care Needs

Health care also became an early concern during the war, as hundreds of injured Iraqis swarmed medical facilities in need of care. However, the fighting damaged many hospitals and other facilities, and those that remained after the U.S. victory were virtually destroyed by looters, who stole essential medical supplies and equipment. Also some facilities did not have electrical power, and medical staff often failed to report to work because of fears for their safety, as law and order evaporated with the fall of the regime. Although Baghdad hospitals coped initially, on April 11 the Red Cross claimed that "the medical system in Baghdad ha[d] virtually collapsed"[52] because of war damage and looting. The Red Cross urged U.S. forces to take control, noting that under the Geneva Conventions, treaties that set out the rules of war, an occupying power is responsible for maintaining order. Outlying areas in Iraq faced similar health crises: In Kurdish-controlled northern Iraq, for example, international humanitarian agencies reported a massive increase in acute respiratory infection and diarrhea.

On May 20 the World Health Organization (WHO) began a program to bring basic health services in Iraq back to

An Iraqi man tends to his brother who lost a leg during the U.S. assault. The fighting damaged many hospitals and left the injured with no place to receive medical care.

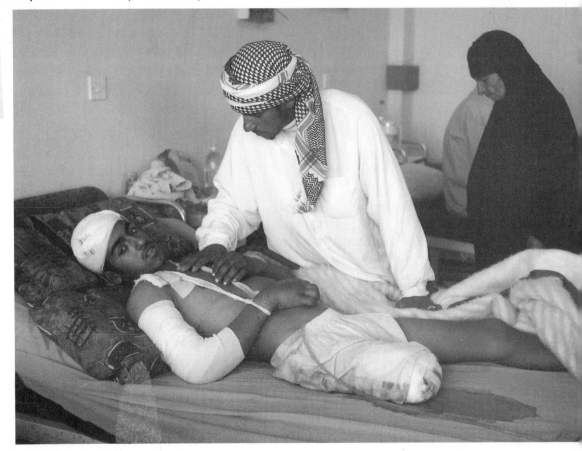

their prewar level, an effort that WHO estimated would cost up to $180 million. The United States, Britain, Spain, and Italy quickly pledged $12 million toward this program. WHO said that it would cost $6.5 million just to make basic structural repairs to correct damage caused by looting; additional funds were needed for medicines, equipment, and paying hospital workers.

President Bush promised to quickly provide necessary humanitarian aid to Iraq. On March 25, as he submitted a request to Congress for funding for the war effort, he said, "This nation and our coalition partners are committed to making sure that the Iraqi citizens who have suffered under a brutal tyrant have got the food and medicine needed as soon as possible."[53] Humanitarian efforts, however, quickly bogged down as the security situation worsened in Iraq. In order to deliver food, repair and restart water treatment facilities, and rebuild health services in Iraq, humanitarian workers need to be able to travel and work within Iraq's borders. This required that they be protected from looters and criminals, a task that U.S. troops were struggling to accomplish during the months following the war's end.

Looting and Chaos

During the war American commanders took great pains to avoid damaging the institutions and infrastructure of Iraq so that Iraq could quickly recover from the war. The sudden defeat of the regime of Saddam Hussein, however, left a gaping power vacuum in the country leading to an unprecedented wave of crime and looting that destroyed much of what the war left standing. Iraqis who suffered under Saddam Hussein's regime sought revenge by destroying government sites; poor Iraqis saw a chance to steal items they desperately needed or could sell for cash; and criminals let loose from Iraqi jails took advantage of the absence of police to commit crimes. As one Iraqi, Mahmoud Ahmed Uthman, described it, "We used to have a brutal dictatorship that controlled everything. . . . When the government collapsed, there was nothing left except a great emptiness. And that emptiness has been filled with chaos."[54]

The looting decimated government buildings, hospitals, museums, universities, banks, businesses, and power and water facilities, gutting them of virtually everything and anything that could be carried off. Critical medical supplies were looted from hospitals, and essential parts were removed from utility facilities. After the initial round of looting, the crime wave continued; armed bands patrolled highways, hijacking private cars and trucks carrying humanitarian supplies, and criminals mugged citizens and burglarized their homes.

Perhaps the worst example of looting was the theft of precious heirlooms and artifacts from Iraq's National Museum in Baghdad. The museum housed some of the world's oldest pieces from ancient Mesopotamia, and experts claimed that major, irreplaceable treasures were stolen, including items such as a lyre from the

Looters flee a government building in Baghdad. The quick collapse of Saddam Hussein's government led to widespread looting in the Iraqi capital.

Sumerian city of Ur dated 2400 B.C. However, museum officials and American investigators later said that although important antiquities were lost, the losses were less serious than originally believed: More than seven hundred artifacts and tens of thousands of ancient manuscripts thought to have been stolen actually had been stored in underground vaults to protect them from the war's damage.

Nevertheless, the loss of many important cultural objects was blamed on the United States. U.S. officials were well aware of the importance of the museum. Experts met with Pentagon officials in January, and the Pentagon provided a memo to military commanders listing the Baghdad museum as the number two priority for protection. The fact that the United States moved quickly to protect the Iraqi Oil Ministry but did not station troops to protect the museum sent a message that the United States valued oil more than Iraq's cultural heritage. As Frank Rich, a columnist for the

An Iraqi man sifts through heirlooms at Baghdad's National Museum. In April 2003, looters ransacked the museum, and many irreplaceable works of art were stolen or destroyed.

New York Times, said, "By protecting Iraq's oil but not its cultural motherlode, we echo the values of no one more than Saddam, who in 1995 cut off funds to the Baghdad museum, pleading the impact of sanctions, yet nonetheless found plenty of money to pour into his own palaces."[55]

One cost of the looting crisis was growing Iraqi anger at the United States and problems for the reconstruction of Iraq. The instability prevented the quick infu-sion of humanitarian aid and slowed the efforts to get Iraq's electricity and other utilities up and running after the war. Karim W. Hassan, director general of Iraq's electricity commission, pleaded, "Give me security and I'll give you electricity."[56] The delays in restoring electricity and telecommunications, in turn, have kept businesses and banks closed and, with armed robbers on the highway, trade and commerce virtually stopped. Once order is restored, the full damage from the looting will be revealed and will result in significantly higher reconstruction costs.

U.S. Unprepared for Chaos

The U.S. military appeared unprepared to stop the postwar chaos. The American prewar expectations envisioned Iraqis cheering the U.S. presence in their country and an easy transition to democracy, using Iraqi police to retain order and Iraqi soldiers to help with rebuilding projects. Perhaps because there was no pay, however, policemen did not return to work and soldiers disappeared, allowing many Iraqis to take advantage of the lack of authority.

Saddam's Mass Graves

After the war ended in Iraq, Iraqis began to discover and dig up mass graves throughout Iraq that contained the bodies of political prisoners who were arrested or disappeared during Saddam Hussein's rule. In many cases, these discoveries are the first information relatives have received about the fates of their missing loved ones.

For example, in Mahawil, a farming area in central Iraq, Iraqis have discovered mass graves containing perhaps eleven thousand bodies. The area is believed to be an execution and gravesite for Shias killed by the government when they rebelled against Hussein's rule in February and March 1991. As Patrick E. Tyler reported on May 15, 2003, in the *New York Times*, "There are signs of blindfolds binding many skulls, which are marked with execution wounds, and some bundles seem to contain the mingled bones of more than one person, perhaps of a mother and child." A similar mass grave was discovered in Habbaniya, fifty miles west of Baghdad, where six hundred corpses were found; these are believed to be the six hundred Kuwaiti prisoners taken by Hussein's security forces when Iraq invaded Kuwait in 1990. The process of digging up and identifying all the victims of Hussein's evil is expected to take a very long time.

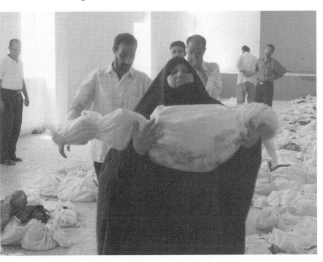

An Iraqi woman carries the body of a family member found in one of Iraq's many mass graves.

In addition, the U.S. military force in Iraq was limited in size, and the U.S. plan was to move troops out of the country as quickly as possible after the war to avoid being seen as an occupier of Arab lands. For example, only about twenty thousand American troops were stationed at the end of the war in Baghdad, a city of about 4.5 million people. Many of those troops had other important responsibilities, such as rooting out remaining pockets of Iraqi fighters, preventing them from patrolling for looters. Also, the troops, equipped only with heavy tanks, were ineffective because they could not maneuver around the city.

Making matters worse, initially the U.S. and British response was to minimize the security problem and avoid using force against looters because of fear that this image would further antagonize the Arab world. Secretary of Defense Rumsfeld spoke of the hands-off attitude that characterized the initial U.S. attitude in a Pentagon briefing: "We've seen looting in this country [referring to the United States]. . . . We've seen riots at soccer games in various countries around the world. . . . To the extent it happens in a war zone, it's difficult to stop."[57]

Instead, Americans sought out Iraqi civic leaders and asked them to take on the task of providing the necessary security. In some areas, as a result of the vacuum of authority, Iraqis began turning to self-appointed authorities. In Baghdad, for example, a man called Muhammad Mohsen Zobeidi openly declared himself mayor and began dispensing decisions until he was arrested by U.S. troops. In other areas tribal leaders and religious leaders tried to take control.

U.S. Efforts to Restore Order

Soon, however, it became clear that security was the first and most important priority for U.S. forces. In April, U.S. troops began joint patrols with Iraqis, including several hundred Iraqi police officers who reported to duty without pay. Later in the month the United States announced that four thousand more troops would be sent to Iraq to help restore order. In perhaps the most significant change, the United States replaced Jay Garner, an American army general charged with overseeing reconstruction, with a civilian administrator—L. Paul Bremer III. His appointment marked a turning point in the postwar administration of Iraq.

Bremer vowed to restore order and emphasized the need for greater numbers of American troops. As a first step he immediately arrested about three hundred violent criminals who had been released by Saddam Hussein, in an effort to demonstrate U.S. resolve. As part of the new, tough security policy, Bremer also authorized U.S. military forces to shoot looters, increased patrols, announced he would hire more police officers, and banned ranking members of the Baath Party from public service. Next he disbanded Iraq's military and the security organizations that supported Saddam Hussein's regime and announced a ban on assault weapons.

Bremer, however, insisted that things in Iraq were not quite as bad as they were

Iraq's new civilian administrator L. Paul Bremer III talks with the press after arriving in Baghdad in May 2003. Bremer vowed to restore order to postwar Iraq.

being portrayed. He stated, "Let's put this in perspective. . . . First of all, this is not a country in anarchy. People are going about their business. They are going about their lives."[58] He said that the U.S. military had started aggressive patrols and that two courts were operating to deal with criminals who are caught, and added: "We have made progress. We are making progress every day, and we [will] continue to make progress in the days ahead."[59]

Nevertheless, months after U.S. troops first entered Baghdad, America was still trying to develop a plan to secure Iraq with far too few troops and a local police force of seven thousand that was just beginning to be reestablished. American soldiers from the Third Infantry Division, which helped to capture Baghdad in the war, were tiring and expecting to go home; instead, however, their mission was extended in Iraq. The United States made plans for a much larger

War Costs and Profits

After months of hedging before the war began, the Bush administration finally revealed the cost of the war to the American people on March 25, after the war had begun. Congress awarded the president approximately $63 billion to cover the cost of war in Iraq and some initial funds for relief and reconstruction. The administration will have to return to Congress to request more money to pay for reconstructing Iraq, and the total cost to American taxpayers is expected to reach at least $100 billion, if not more.

If ordinary taxpayers lost money on the war, however, certain other Americans stood to make large profits. Indeed, corporations connected with the Bush administration and the U.S. military were awarded big contracts for rebuilding Iraq even before the war started. For example, before the war, the Army Corps of Engineers awarded a $7 billion, two-year contract to fight oil fires to a subsidiary of Halliburton, the company Vice President Dick Cheney ran from 1995 to 2000. As soon as the war ended, on April 17, the Bush administration awarded the Bechtel Group of San Francisco a major contract for reconstructing Iraq. This contract will initially pay Bechtel $34.6 million and could eventually be worth as much as $680 million over a period of eighteen

months. The total cost of rebuilding is expected to cost some $20 billion a year for the next three years, according to some experts. Bechtel is connected to former Secretary of State George Shultz, who serves on its board of directors and is also on the board of the Committee for the Liberation of Iraq, a group with close ties to the White House that had lobbied in favor of the war.

These contract awards to Washington insiders were heavily criticized because they suggest favoritism for Bush friends. As an April 14, 2003, editorial in the *New York Times* put it, "This looks like naked favoritism and undermines the Bush administration's portrayal of the war as a campaign for disarmament and democracy, not [monetary gain]." In fact, the Halliburton contract was awarded without allowing any other competing companies to bid, bypassing federal contracting regulations. Similarly, the Bechtel contract was awarded without offering coalition allies, such as Britain, or other countries the opportunity to bid for the vast reconstruction work. U.S. officials, however, have promised to allow companies from other countries to submit bids for subcontracting work. This was not enough for the U.S. Congress, which began an investigation of the matter.

force in Iraq than originally anticipated; about 150,000 U.S. troops were committed to Iraq as of June, and many believed that number was likely to increase. The United States also has asked about seventy other countries to contribute troops to

the postwar effort, and as of July 2003, twenty-four had committed to do so. Countries sending troops included Hungary, Bulgaria, Honduras, El Salvador, Ukraine, Slovakia, Denmark, and Spain, with some countries sending only a few hundred troops and others sending one to two thousand.

As months passed, the United States came under growing criticism for not anticipating the need for security in postwar Iraq. U.S. senators, for example, assailed Deputy Defense Secretary Paul D. Wolfowitz with criticisms in a meeting of the Senate Foreign Relations Committee on May 22. Senator Richard G. Lugar, a Republican who heads the committee, said, "I am concerned that the administration's initial stabilization and reconstruction efforts have been inadequate.

... The planning for peace was much less developed than the planning for war."[60] Similarly, political columnist Thomas Friedman, in an editorial in the *New York Times*, wrote that the United States is "not only underestimating how hard nation building will be with this brutalized people, but how much the looting and power vacuum have put us into an even deeper hole."[61] Friedman, among with many others hoping for a positive outcome to the situation, urged that America's attention must not be diverted from the postwar needs of Iraq.

Chapter Five

Challenges for the New Iraq

A merica's vision for a new Iraq is a prosperous economy fueled in large part by Iraq's vast oil wealth, a secular democratic government in which ethnic and religious groups share power, and a modern, educated, and free society that creates a shining example for other Arab nations in the Middle East. The Iraq that emerged as of June 2003, however, was a country very much in transition, still in disorder, angry about its occupation by foreigners, and only beginning a long struggle toward democracy and prosperity. As a result, the United States had to shelve its early, optimistic plans for a rapid reconstruction, power transition, and troop pullout to accept that the birthing of a new Iraq would be a much longer, harder, and more dangerous job, for both Americans and Iraqis. As *New York Times* columnist Thomas L. Friedman put it,

Friends, whether you like or hate how and why we got into this war, the fact is America . . . has assumed responsibility for rebuilding Iraq. We are talking about one of the biggest nation-building projects the U.S. has ever undertaken, the mother of all long hauls. We now have a 51st state of 23 million people. We just adopted a baby called Baghdad . . . [and] raising that baby, in the neighborhood it lives in, is going to be a mammoth task.[62]

The Delay of Iraqi Self-Rule

The United States, in keeping with its goal of avoiding the "occupier" label in Iraq and turning over power to Iraqis as quickly as possible, initially projected that a transitional Iraqi government would be formed shortly after the war's end.

The first meeting with various Iraqi factions to discuss forming a provisional government for Iraq was held on April 15 in the southern city of Ur. It included all three ethnic groups (Kurds, Sunnis, and Shias) from inside Iraq as well as Iraqis who had spent years in exile. Thousands of Shia Muslims, however, boycotted the gathering as a protest against the American military occupation of Iraq. The meeting produced a thirteen-point communique declaring, among other things, that the new Iraq must be democratic and that Saddam's Baath Party must be dissolved.

A second general meeting was held on April 28, Saddam Hussein's sixty-sixth birthday. Like the first meeting, it attracted delegates from inside and outside Iraq, including Shiite and Sunni Muslim clerics, Kurds from the north, Arab tribal chiefs, and Iraqi exiles. The group, with U.S. encouragement, decided at this time to hold a national conference

A man speaks at the April 28, 2003, general meeting during which representatives from Iraq's many political and ethnic groups voted to hold a national conference to select a transitional government.

in May 2003 to select a "transitional government" for Iraq, a term referring to an Iraq-led interim governing body. Under this plan, fully approved by the United States, Iraqis were to be quickly granted governing power over Iraq. Former U.S. administrator Jay Garner promised, "Next week, or by the second week in May [2003], you'll see the beginning of a nucleus of a temporary Iraqi government, a government with an Iraqi face on it that is totally dealing with the coalition."[63]

In mid-May, however, the United States and Britain abruptly reversed their plans for quickly turning over control to an Iraqi transitional government. Instead, L. Paul Bremer, the new American administrator, announced on May 16 that the coalition would remain in charge of Iraq for an indefinite period. In making the announcement, Bremer explained that a U.S.-led "interim authority" could assist Iraq in creating a constitution and developing democratic elections and that the delay would allow time to broaden participation in the Iraqi leadership. John Sawers, a British diplomat representing British prime minister Tony Blair, however, suggested that the allies

Demonstrators take to the streets of Baghdad in May 2003 to protest the prolonged American occupation of Iraq after the war.

delayed the hand-over of power to Iraqis because of fear that that a divided or weak interim government, given the continuing disorder, could not control Iraq. He said, "It's quite clear that you cannot transfer all powers onto some interim body, because it will not have the strength or the resources to carry those responsibilities out."[64]

Iraqi Anger over the Delay

For their part, Iraqis were greatly disappointed with the decision. "I don't think they trust this group [referring to the initial group of Iraqi political factions that emerged in Iraq] to function as a political leadership,"[65] said one Iraqi political figure. Others expressed stronger anger over the decision. Adel Abdel Mahdi, political adviser to the Supreme Council for the Islamic Revolution, one of Iraq's largest Shia political groups, for example, openly accused the United States of reneging on promises to support the rapid creation of an Iraqi-led interim government. His comments reflected the disappointment felt by many other groups, including Kurdish political groups and the Iraqi National Congress. On May 25, in one of the strongest shows of dissatisfaction, an estimated ten thousand Shia Muslims protested in Baghdad, demanding that the United States turn over power to an Iraqi government and withdraw its troops from the country.

That same day, several of the main Iraqi political groups, who call themselves the "leadership council," decided to submit a formal protest to U.S. authorities complaining about the delay in setting up an Iraqi government. They also planned to send delegations to Washington and London to lobby for quick elections. The leadership council comprises groups such the two main Kurdish factions in northern Iraq, the Iraqi National Congress of Ahmad Chalabi, the Iraqi National Accord of Iyad Alawi, the Shiite Muslim movement of Ayatollah Muhammad Bakr al-Hakim, the Shiite Dawa Party, and the democratic movement of Nasir al-Chadirchy.

Following the Iraqi complaints, as part of an effort to involve Iraqis in decision-making, Bremer met with Iraqi political groups and promised to hold a national conference in July to create an interim Iraqi political council of twenty-five to thirty Iraqis to help administer the country. Bremer also agreed to hold a national conference to appoint an all-Iraqi commission that would be charged with drafting a new constitution for Iraq. These Iraqi bodies, however, would not be independent but would operate under U.S. authority.

However, the Iraqi leadership council continued to criticize Bremer's plans. In response to the leadership council's demands, Bremer modified his original plan for an interim Iraqi political council by agreeing to give the council more power in naming ministers to an interim administration and in making recommendations for a new currency, oil production, economic strategy, and education reform. Nevertheless, one of the leadership council's main political factions and a leading Shia Muslim party, the Supreme Council for the Islamic Revolution of Iraq, announced

Shiite Abdul Aziz al-Hakim (left), Iraqi National Congress leader Ahmad Chalabi (third from left), former foreign minister Adnan Pachichi (facing page, left), and Kurdish leader Jalal Talibani (facing page, right) from Iraq's main political groups formed the Leadership Council in an effort to restore self-rule in Iraq.

that it would not join Bremer's Iraqi political council if its members were appointed by Americans.

Bremer also encountered trouble for his plan for a constitutional commission. On June 30, Iraq's leading moderate Shia cleric, Grand Ayatollah Ali al-Sistani, issued a fatwa, or religious ruling, rejecting the idea of an American-controlled constitutional commission, arguing that Iraqis should elect the drafters of their constitution. Despite the difficulties Bremer was encountering, however, it seemed clear that Iraqi political groups, at least temporarily, had lost the chance to take full control of postwar Iraq.

UN Approval of the American Occupation

The United States, simultaneously, was seeking UN support for a resolution that would both legitimize U.S. authority over postwar Iraq and lift UN economic sanc-

tions on Iraq. On May 22 the UN Security Council voted unanimously to allow the United States and Britain to occupy and rebuild Iraq and to end nearly thirteen years of sanctions. The resolution also gave a limited role to a United Nations special representative to help create a new Iraqi government; Sergio Vieira de Mello, a long-time UN executive, was chosen for this position.

The UN vote was a significant diplomatic victory for the Bush administration, because France, Germany, and Russia, who strongly opposed the war in Iraq, agreed to support the resolution and to accept almost complete U.S. control of postwar Iraq. Indeed, the effect of the vote was to give the United States and Britain control, not only over Iraq's political development, but also over its billions of dollars in annual oil revenues. U.S. officials had been anxious to get Iraq's oil flowing and have promised that these oil revenues will be used to finance

reconstruction in Iraq. The U.S. power over Iraq, according to the terms of the resolution, will expire when an internationally recognized representative government takes power in Iraq, a goal that may take several years to reach.

Reconstruction and Rebuilding the Iraqi Oil Industry

In addition to the political challenges that come with the deposing of a twenty-four-year-long authoritarian regime and the creation of a democracy where none has ever existed before, U.S. administrators also face the huge job of rebuilding Iraq's economy. The Baath Party's pillage of Iraq's wealth, combined with years of economic sanctions and several wars, left the country's economy shattered. Fixing it will require not only restoration of basic services and infrastructure (such as roads, bridges, and buildings) but also the rebuilding of important Iraqi industries, especially its oil industry.

Reconstruction began early after the war ended but was expected to take some time. Bechtel, the American company that

was awarded the first main reconstruction contract, immediately began working to repair electrical and other services. It quickly had potential subcontractors from all over the world lining up to bid for the various subcontracts necessary for other reconstruction efforts. Some of these early reconstruction efforts were frustrated, however, by looters who stole necessary repair items such as copper cable used for electrical wiring in high-tension power lines. In addition, because the problems in Iraq were more serious than first anticipated, the United States decided to focus on emergency repairs rather than on major reconstruction of Iraq's crumbling electricity and water and sanitation systems. Later, Bechtel hopes to persuade U.S. officials and legislators to undertake more comprehensive water, sewage, and electricity rebuilding projects.

Another step important to reviving Iraq's economy was acquiring financing to pay for reconstruction and rebuilding. In late May, U.S. administrator Bremer announced the opening of bank credit lines to allow Iraq to pay for goods and services essential to its reconstruction. In addition, U.S. administrators expect some Iraqi cash to help pay for reconstruction costs. Fortunately American troops have recovered close to $1 billion believed to have been stolen from Iraq's Central Bank just before the war by Saddam Hussein's son, Qusay. U.S. forces later discovered another $250 million in American currency in the flooded basement vault of the Central Bank.

Yet another important economic priority to help pay for reconstruction was restoring the country's oil production. The end of sanctions will allow Iraq to export oil more freely than under Hussein's regime and should eventually bring in a sizable income for Iraq. Thanks to U.S. efforts and the work of talented Iraqi oil engineers and

Iraq's Oil

Iraq's southern fields are among the largest of Iraq's oil reserves and were among the first areas secured by U.S. forces when the war began. Experts predicted the southern Rumeila oil field, for example, could produce up to 1.1 million barrels a day within weeks after the end of the war. Total oil production in Iraq, according to the Iraqi Oil Ministry, could reach the country's prewar output of 2 to 3 million barrels a day in about eighteen months.

As of the end of May 2003, however, the postwar Iraqi oil production was still only a fraction of its prewar level due to damage to refineries and pipelines. Indeed, production was so low that, in a country awash in oil, the U.S. military was forced to truck in more than a million gallons of gasoline a day just to meet the country's domestic needs.

Meanwhile, the issue of who will control Iraqi oil has yet to be resolved. Under a May 22, 2003, United Nations resolution, the United States was given broad authority over Iraq's economy, including its oil industry. However, prior to the vote on the resolution, the U.S. administration set up an oil advisory team, comprised of both Iraqis and Americans, that was to be responsible for running the country's oil industry. On May 3, U.S. officials named two Iraqi oil officials and a former American oil executive to this team. This advisory group will likely make important decisions such as whether Iraq's oil industry will be owned by private companies or the government and whether foreign companies will be permitted such ownership rights.

The issue of who will control and own Iraqi oil is highly controversial and very important to both Iraqis and U.S. officials, because there is a widespread belief in Iraq and throughout the Arab world that one of the main motives behind the U.S. war was for America to get control of Iraq's vast oil reserves. As columnist and TV commentator Rami G. Khouri explained in a May 19, 2003, article in *Maclean's*, "Most analysts and ordinary citizens believe the U.S. wants to control Iraq's oil, secure a permanent Mideast military foothold from which to dominate and pacify the region, and reduce the incidence of terror emanating from the area." The failure to turn up weapons of mass destruction, which was President Bush's main justification for going to war, has made critics of America even more suspicious about whether the United States will try to take over Iraq's oil. Nevertheless, U.S. officials promised that Iraqi oil belongs to Iraqis. Whether that promise will be kept has yet to be shown.

On June 22, 2003, these two oil tankers became the first to export Iraqi oil since the war began. Here, the tankers wait at a terminal in Turkey to unload 2 million barrels of oil.

technicians, oil began flowing, both from Iraq's southern fields and from oil fields in northern Iraq in May. On June 22, Iraq exported its first oil since the end of the war. However, steady oil exports were delayed because of severe looting and sabotage of oil facilities during the months following the war. As a result, production as of early July 2003 leveled off at roughly eight hundred thousand barrels a day, significantly less than the prewar goal of 2 to 3 million barrels a day.

Restoring Jobs

Another critical challenge for U.S. officials in Iraq was providing jobs and getting the economy moving. The war and postwar chaos all but destroyed business activity in Iraq, and U.S. administrators disbanded the country's largest employer—the government—leaving thousands of workers unemployed. For example, about 100,000 Iraqi soldiers and civilians lost their jobs when American officials dissolved the

Ministries of Defense and Information, approximately 250,000 people used to work for government ministries that no longer are functioning, as many as 96,000 workers were idled from Iraq's state-owned businesses, and an additional 60,000 people are now unemployed who worked for Iraq's military and weapons companies.

In the face of protests and threats of suicide bombings from unemployed army and government workers, U.S. administrator Bremer announced a $70 million temporary jobs program that would pay Iraqis low wages to collect trash and rebuild schools. He also promised to recruit ex-soldiers for a new Iraqi army, as long as they were not Baath Party officers. In addition, the Iraqi government, with U.S. permission, began making payments to about two hundred thousand military officers and paying full salaries to approximately 1.3 million employees of government ministries and Iraq's government-owned companies, even though there was no work for them to do. As for business activity, many stores and small businesses in Baghdad reopened in May, although many closed early because of fears that they would be robbed after dark by looters and thieves.

U.S. soldiers hand out application forms for the new Iraqi army. Offering Iraqis jobs in the new army was part of Bremer's efforts to rebuild Iraq's stalled economy.

Encouraging Business Investment

Ultimately, rebuilding Iraq's economy will require individuals and businesses to invest in Iraqi companies. U.S. administrator Bremer indicated that America's priority is to shift Iraq's economy from the state industries to the private sector. Closing state industries that are losing money will be difficult because of the hardships that would be created for their employees who would lose their jobs, but the U.S. officials believe such actions will be necessary to attract investment and make industry in Iraq competitive in the world economy.

Experts expect that small entrepreneurs are likely to be the first to invest in Iraq's economy. Eventually, however, as security improves, experts predict that bigger companies and foreign investors will see the advantage of investing in business opportunities in the new Iraq. Some of these investors may come from a small group of Iraqi merchant families who existed even before Saddam Hussein's rule and who remain very wealthy today.

Experts warn, however, that investors in the new Iraq should be prepared to weather many challenges, not only immediate ones such as lack of power, difficulties with communication and transportation, and the updating of equipment, but also longer-range problems such as an expected increase in imports. Iraq's businesses have been weakened by many disadvantages over a long period of time, including UN economic sanctions, Hussein's bad management, outdated equipment, and a lack of marketing skills. In the new Iraq the relaxation of import restrictions will add a new challenge—a veritable landslide of international companies who will want to sell their products to Iraqis and compete with Iraqi companies. As of July 2003, however, these concerns were not an issue because investors considered Iraq to be still too unstable for them to make major financial commitments.

Preventing a Baath Party Resurgence

As American forces fought to restore order, they began to face two new threats to security in postwar Iraq—a spate of increasingly serious sniper and hit-and-run guerrilla attacks on U.S. and British soldiers and incidents of sabotage on oil pipelines, the Baghdad electrical system, a liquid natural gas plant, and other important infrastructure sites. Most of the attacks on soldiers occurred in central Iraq, considered to be a stronghold of former members of the Baath Party.

The guerrilla attacks and sabotage, although not a serious threat to military forces, greatly increased the insecurity of investors about Iraq, made life more difficult for Iraqis, and caused military casualties at a time when Americans at home believed the war was over. Indeed, the numbers of U.S. soldiers killed in Iraq since May 1, the day President Bush declared major combat over, eventually exceeded the number killed during the war.

U.S. officials attributed the attacks on soldiers to remnants of the Baath Party of

Saddam Hussein and members of the Saddam Fedayeen paramilitary force. The sabotage incidents also appeared to be the work of pro-Saddam loyalists. These attacks were believed to be part of a plan prepared by Hussein's government before the war, based on a document found in the southern Iraqi city of Basra dated January 23 and purportedly prepared by the Iraqi Intelligence Service. The document called for a sabotage campaign in case Hussein's regime was overthrown and outlined various types of sabotage, such as looting and burning government offices, sabotaging power plants, cutting communication lines, and attacking water purification plants.

The American administrator of Iraq, L. Paul Bremer III, vowed that the attacks would not deter U.S. efforts to reconstruct Iraq: "We're certainly not panicked," he said, "We're not going to get deflected from our direction by an attack now and then, tragic as it may be."[66] In response to the guerrilla attacks, the United States stepped up patrols, conducted more house-to-house searches, and in late June carried out an aggressive series of raids, seeking to root out and intimidate the troublemakers. Troops arrested numerous Iraqis and seized some weapons and documents but as of July 2003 had not uncovered any major pockets of resistance. This heightened military response, unfortunately, only increased resentment among ordinary Iraqis toward the American occupation.

Also, as of fall 2003, although U.S. forces located and killed his two sons, most believed that Hussein was still alive and in hiding in Iraq, waiting to stage a coup if the U.S. effort to govern the country faltered. Experts admit that Hussein's party has a long history of survival and self-preservation, as well as experience in working underground and in secret. As Saad Obeidi, a psychological warfare specialist assisting the American military, explains,

> Time has always been the backbone of Saddam's strategy. He is a man who knows the psychology and sociology of Iraq. The looting and disorder we see now fall in his favor. Americans have to act fast. People will forget all about the Baath Party if order and prosperity return.[67]

In an effort to help prevent a resurgence of Hussein and his Baath Party, the U.S. administrator in Iraq banned between fifteen and thirty thousand Baath Party officials from participation in any future Iraqi government. In addition, the United States disbanded the armed forces, the Republican Guard, the Defense Ministry, and the Information Ministry, all of which supported the most repressive activities of Hussein's regime. However, it is not proving easy to get rid of Baath Party officials. Often, these people are the only ones with expertise, and as a result senior party officials were often hired by U.S. authorities in their efforts to stabilize Iraq.

As might be expected, these appointments drew protests from local Iraqis. For example, in early May hundreds of Iraqi doctors, nurses, and health workers de-

An Iraqi child heaves a rock at a burning U.S. army vehicle that was destroyed by a guerrilla attack in Baghdad.

monstrated against the U.S. appointment of Ali al-Janabi, a senior Baath Party member, to be minister of health for Iraq. Similar protests occurred at other Iraqi ministries. The cost of "de-Baathification," it seemed, would be not only the loss of American lives fighting former Baath Party members but also the loss of some of the country's most able administrators.

Bridging Iraq's Ethnic and Religious Differences

In addition to uprooting Baath Party loyalists, American administrators worry that the overthrow of Saddam Hussein will lead

An American soldier passes an army truck ambushed by guerrillas. U.S. officials attribute most of the guerrilla attacks to Baath Party loyalists and the Saddam Fedayeen paramilitary force.

to renewed religious and ethnic strife among Iraq's other ethnic groups. Disagreements between the three groups—the Kurds, Shias, and Sunnis—were controlled during Hussein's rule largely because Sunnis held complete power and brutally repressed the two other sects. Since the end of the war, however, the absence of a government or other strong authority has led not only Hussein's Sunni loyalists but also the two other ethnic groups to defend their ethnic identities and compete for power in postwar Iraq.

Since the war's end, for example, the Kurds have been returning to the cities and towns where they grew up, leading to ethnic clashes with Arab residents that were located into Kurdish areas by Saddam Hussein. Hussein's brutal ethnic cleansing campaigns in the 1970s and 1980s threw many Kurdish citizens out of their homes and brought in Arabs to replace them; in this way Hussein acquired control over the rich oil resources of northern Iraq. In the first months after the war, Kurds reclaimed the major northern cities of Kirkuk and

Mosul and hundreds of other towns and villages. Kurds even felt safe enough to return to Halabja, a town that Hussein had attacked with chemical weapons in 1988. The returning Kurds, however, have been confronting Arabs, leading to ethnic clashes and gunfights. In May, for example, fighting in Kirkuk left nine people dead. In addition, Kurdish leaders announced that they would force Arabs who came to northern cities during Saddam Hussein's rule to leave those areas.

The Shias (or Shiites), who make up almost two-thirds of Iraq's population but who have long been persecuted by Hussein's Sunni government, have also been jousting for power since the war ended. The Shias share the Islamic religion but, in the postwar period, divisions between different Shia religious leaders have resulted in confrontations and violence. In April, for example, Sheik Abdel Majid al-Khoei, a well-known Shia cleric, was murdered by a mob just days after he returned to Iraq from exile.

Confrontations also have taken place between the followers of other rival clerics who are competing for political power.

A Kurdish man in Kirkunarab (left) is forced from his home ny the Kurdish man on the right. Displaced Kurds have reclaimed Kirkuk and other towns Saddam Husseim forced them to abandon.

Until he was killed by a bomb blast in August 2003 Ayatollah Muhammad Bakr al-Hakim lead the Supreme Council of the Islamic Revolution in Iraq, one of the most popular Shia groups in Iraq. Another popular cleric whose followers often protested Hakim's appearances was Moktada al-Sadr, a thirty-year-old who emerged shortly after the fall of Baghdad. Both Ayatollah Hakim and Sadr are opposed to the American presence in Iraq and seek to create an Islamic government in Iraq. Other more moderate Shia leaders, although less prominent, are believed to favor a separation of religion and government.

The U.S. hope is that a democratic government can be created in Iraq that allows all three main ethnic groups to share power and that separates religion from government. The fear of many, however, is that the majority of Shias might try to create an Islamic government that imposes fundamentalist Muslim religious values as state policy. This could upset U.S. support and alienate other powerful tribal and ethnic leaders that will be important for a stable and united Iraq.

The Future of Iraq

Around the world and in Iraq, reaction to the U.S.-led war and the overthrow of Saddam Hussein's regime varied, but the one point most seemed to agree on was that the United States should leave Iraq as soon as possible, leaving Iraqis the freedom to govern themselves. The United States appeared to share this vision and initially planned for a quick turnover of power to

Kurdish Hopes for Independence

Because of historic persecution at the hands of Hussein and others, the Kurds have long strived for an independent Kurdish state. With American protection, they have successfully governed their own independent region in northern Iraq since the time of the first Persian Gulf war in 1991.

For practical and political reasons, Kurdish political leaders have agreed to become part of the new Iraq, but most Kurdish people would prefer a separate Kurdish nation. Barham Salih, governor of the eastern Kurdish enclave, in a 2003 *New York Times* article explained,

No Kurd can dissuade himself of the right to self-determination, but . . . we know the possibility of a Kurdish state in Iraq is a very distant one. The tangible thing for us is to work for a federal democracy and be a full-fledged Iraqi citizen.

Kurdish leaders, therefore, have been working with American forces and can be expected to be an influential voice in any new Iraqi government. There is a fear, however, that they could seek to break away from Iraq if Iraq's new government does not provide them with security and some measure of self-rule.

an Iraqi interim authority and a quick pull-out of U.S. troops. However, the reality of postwar Iraq soon changed U.S. plans. Disorder continued and obstacles to reconstruction mounted, making it clear that the United States would have to stay in Iraq longer than expected. To do otherwise would risk anarchy, which could result in either the return of Saddam Hussein or the rise to power of yet another strongman like him. Such a result would negate the struggle to liberate Iraq and condemn it to even more suffering.

Therefore, it appeared that Iraq's future would be a period of difficult transition and that the United States would be responsible for Iraq for some time to come. For Iraqis already chafing under the U.S. and British occupation, this was not welcome news. If, however, the United States can withstand the pressure from critics, actually improve the lives of Iraqis, and help them create a government that promises real freedom, the United States may yet claim the mantle of "liberator," and Iraq's future may, indeed, turn bright.

Notes

Introduction: Winning the Peace

1. Thomas L. Friedman, "Because We Could," *New York Times*, June 4, 2003.

Chapter One:
Iraq's History of Aggression and Arms

2. Geoff Simons, *Iraq: From Sumer to Saddam.* New York: St. Martin's, 1994, p. 178.
3. Said K. Aburish, *Saddam Hussein, The Politics of Revenge.* New York: Bloomsbury, 2000, p. 2.
4. Simons, *Iraq: From Sumer to Saddam,* p. 231.
5. Quoted in Simons, *Iraq: From Sumer to Saddam,* p. 246.
6. Simons, *Iraq: From Sumer to Saddam,* p. 233.
7. Quoted in Aburish, *Saddam Hussein, The Politics of Revenge,* p. 100.
8. Simons, *Iraq: From Sumer to Saddam,* p. 249.
9. Quoted in Dilip Hiro, *The Longest War: The Iran-Iraq Military Conflict.* New York: Routledge Chapman & Hall, 1991, p. 35.
10. Con Coughlin, *Saddam: King of Terror.* New York: HarperCollins, 2002, p. 238.
11. Coughlin, *Saddam: King of Terror,* p. 255.
12. Quoted in Coughlin, *Saddam: King of Terror,* p. 256.
13. Coughlin, *Saddam: King of Terror,* p. 263.
14. The White House, "A Decade of Deception and Defiance," September 12, 2002. http://usinfo.state.gov.

Chapter Two: The Axis of Evil and Diplomatic Efforts to Disarm Iraq

15. George W. Bush, Address to a Joint Session of Congress and the Nation, Washington, DC, September 20, 2001. www.white house. gov.
16. George W. Bush, President's State of the Union Address, Washington, DC, January 29, 2002. www.whitehouse. gov.
17. Bush, President's State of the Union Address.
18. Bush, President's State of the Union Address.
19. Dick Cheney, speech to the Veterans of Foreign Wars 103rd National Convention, August 26, 2002. www.whitehouse. gov.
20. Richard Butler, Statement at the Senate Foreign Relations Committee, Washington, DC, July 31, 2002. www.iraqwatch.org.
21. Quoted in William Safire, "Clear Ties of Terror," *New York Times*, January 27, 2003.
22. Al Gore, speech to the Commonwealth Club, San Fransisco, September 9, 2002. www.gore2004us.com.
23. David R. Gergen, "It's Time to Speak Loudly," *U.S. News & World Report,* August 19, 2002.
24. Quoted in *New York Times*, "Interview with Jacques Chirac," September 9, 2002.
25. George W. Bush, speech to the United Nations, New York, September 12, 2002. www.whitehouse. gov.
26. Resolution 1441, adopted by the United Nations at Security Council meeting 4644, November 8, 2002. www.cnn.com.
27. Resolution 1441.
28. Quoted in United Nations, United Nations Monitoring, Verification and Inspection Commission, Notes for Briefing the Security Council, January 9, 2003. www.un.org.

29. Colin Powell, speech to the United Nations, New York, February 5, 2003. www.state.gov.
30. Powell, speech to the United Nations.
31. Draft Resolution on Iraq by the United States, Great Britain, and Spain, circulated to the UN Security Council on February 23, 2003. www.cnn.com.
32. Quoted in *Associated Press*, "Bush Warns Allies Against Inaction in Confronting Baghdad," January 21, 2003.
33. Quoted in *Associated Press*, "Bush Warns Allies Against Inaction in Confronting Baghdad."
34. Memo submitted to United Nations Security Council by France, Germany, and Russia on February 24, 2003. www.cnn.com.
35. George W. Bush, speech to the nation, March 17, 2003. www.whitehouse.gov.

Chapter Three:
Shock and Awe in Twenty-Six Days

36. Quoted in Marc Santora, "From Hussein, Defiance and Praise for His Troops," *New York Times*, March 24, 2003.
37. *New York Times*, "A New War," March 24, 2003.
38. Quoted in Jim Dwyer, "A Gulf Commander Sees a Longer Road," *New York Times*, March 28, 2003.
39. Quoted in R.W. Apple Jr., "Bush Moves to Prepare Public for a Harder War," *New York Times*, March 24, 2003.
40. Quoted in Patrick E. Tyler, "U.S. Tanks Make Quick Strike into Baghdad," *New York Times*, April 6, 2003.
41. Dick Cheney, speech at the American Society of Newspaper Editors, New Orleans, April 9, 2003. www.command-post.org.
42. Quoted in John M. Broder, "'Today the Regime Is in Disarray,' U.S. Commander Says," *New York Times*, April 9, 2003.
43. Quoted in David E. Sanger and Thom Shanker, "Bush Says Regime in Iraq Is No More; Syria Is Penalized," *New York Times*, April 15, 2003.
44. Quoted in Dexter Filkins, "Hunting Hussein, U.S. Attacks Mosque," *New York Times*, April 11, 2003.
45. Quoted in Warren Hoge, "A Letter Said to Be from Saddam Hussein Urges Iraqis to Rebel," *New York Times*, April 30, 2003.
46. *New York Times*, "The Quest for Illicit Weapons," April 18, 2003.
47. Quoted in David E. Sanger, "Viewing the War as a Lesson to the World," *New York Times*, April 5, 2003.
48. Quoted in Christopher Marquis, "World's View of U.S. Sours After Iraq War, Poll Finds," *New York Times*, June 4, 2003.

Chapter Four:
The Aftermath of War in Iraq

49. *Associated Press*, "Partial Count Finds Many Civilians Killed," *San Diego Union-Tribune*, June 11, 2003.
50. *Economist (US)*, "The Other Battle; Humanitarian Assistance," April 5, 2003.
51. *Economist (US)*, "The Other Battle."
52. Quoted in *Reuters*, "Red Cross Urges U.S. to Secure Baghdad's Hospitals," April 11, 2003.
53. George W. Bush, remarks at the Pentagon, Washington, DC, March 25, 2003. www.whitehouse. gov.
54. Quoted in Edmund L. Andrews and Susan Sachs, "Iraq's Slide into Lawlessness Squanders Good Will for U.S.," *New York Times*, May 17, 2003.
55. Frank Rich, "And Now: 'Operation Iraqi Looting,'" *New York Times*, April 28, 2003.

56. Quoted in Andrews and Sachs, "Iraq's Slide into Lawlessness Squanders Good Will for U.S."

57. Quoted in Maureen Dowd, "History up in Smoke," *New York Times*, April 16, 2003.

58. Terence Neilan, "Bremer Says U.S. Is Tackling Security Problem in Baghdad," *New York Times*, May 15, 2003.

59. Terence Neilan, "Bremer Says U.S. is Tackling Security Problem in Baghdad."

60. Quoted in Eric Schmitt, "Senators Sharply Criticize Iraq Rebuilding Efforts," *New York Time*, May 22, 2003.

61. Thomas L. Friedman, "Iraq Fast Becoming Yesterday's Story," *New York Times*, May 22, 2003.

Chapter Five:
Challenges for the New Iraq

62. Thomas L. Friedman, "Our New Baby," *New York Times*, May 12, 2003.

63. Quoted in Patrick E. Tyler, "Opposition Groups to Help to Create Assembly in Iraq," *New York Times*, May 5, 2003.

64. Quoted in Patrick E. Tyler, "In Reversal, Plan for Iraq Self-Rule Has Been Put Off," *New York Times*, May 15, 2003.

65. Tyler, "In Reversal, Plan for Iraq Self-Rule Has Been Put Off."

66. Neela Banerjee, "Marching in Baghdad, Thousands of Shiites Protest Against the U.S.," *New York Times*, May 20, 2003.

67. Quoted in Amy Waldman, "Bremer Says More Attacks Won't Deter the Allies," *New York Times*, June 29, 2003.

Chronology

3100 B.C.
The ancient civilization of Sumer is founded and develops systems of irrigation, trade, and writing.

A.D. 1533–1534
Iraq is conquered by the Ottoman Empire.

1920
Iraq is created in its current boundaries as a British colonial monarchy.

1932
Iraq becomes a sovereign state.

1958
Iraq becomes a republic. The monarchy is overthrown in a military coup led by General Karim Qasim.

1968
The Baath Party seizes power in Iraq; Saddam Hussein's cousin Bakr becomes president; Hussein arises as a key leader in the Party.

1974–1975
Kurds rebel, with the backing of the shah of Iran. Saddam Hussein instrumental in suppressing a Kurdish rebellion by negotiating an end to Iranian support for the Kurds. In exchange Iraq agrees to share sovereignty of the Shatt al-Arab waterway, which provides access to the Persian Gulf.

1979
Saddam Hussein becomes president, purges all opposition through terror.

September 22 Iraq attacks Iran, Iran-Iraq War begins.

1984
United Nations (UN) investigators report that Iraq uses mustard gas and the nerve gas Tabun against Iranians in Iran-Iraq War.

1987
August 20 A UN ceasefire goes into effect to end the Iran-Iraq War.

1988
Saddam Hussein uses chemical weapons against civilian Kurds in the town of Halabja, leaving five thousand dead and ten thousand wounded, and destroying thousands of villages.

1990
August 2 Iraq invades Kuwait. The UN Security Council unanimously passes Resolution 660, condemning the invasion and demanding unconditional and immediate withdrawal.

August 6 The UN Security Council passes Resolution 661, imposing economic sanctions.

November 29 The Security Council passes Resolution 678, authorizing member states to use force unless Iraq leaves Kuwait by January 15, 1991.

1991
April 4 The UN Security Council passes Resolution 687, creating the United Nations Special Committee on Iraq (UNSCOM) to monitor and verify Iraqi compliance with UN disarmament requirements, and requiring the certified destruction of Iraq's weapons of mass destruction as a condition for ending economic sanctions.

1995
Hussein Kamel al-Majid, who headed Iraq's weapons of mass destruction program, defects,

and the world learns that Iraq had a large biological weapons program and had weaponized some biological agents.

1997

Saddam Hussein declares several weapons inspections sites to be "presidential" and therefore off-limits to UNSCOM.

October 31 Saddam Hussein announces his refusal to allow any further UN weapons inspections; UNSCOM reports that it has made "significant progress" in disarming Iraq.

1999

Throughout 1999 and 2000, the United States and Britain pursue an aggressive bombing campaign against Iraq under leadership of President Clinton.

2001

September 11 U.S. World Trade Center attacked by terrorists belonging to Arab terrorist group al-Qaeda, headed by Osama bin Laden. Later, reports surface of a meeting in Prague earlier in 2001 between suicide hijacker Mohammed Atta and an Iraqi intelligence agent, but this is not confirmed. No other evidence of Iraqi complicity in September 11 attack emerges.

2002

January 29 U.S. president Bush announces in State of the Union speech that Iraq is one of three countries forming an "axis of evil," threatening the world by supporting terrorists and developing weapons of mass destruction. Thereafter, U.S. president Bush and administration officials repeatedly make comments indicating support for regime change in Iraq, while European allies and Arab states indicate strong opposition to any attack on Iraq.

September 12 U.S. president Bush addresses the United Nations, outlining Hussein's disregard for multiple UN resolutions, and asking for UN help with Iraqi threat of weapons of mass destruction.

November 8 The UN passes Resolution 1441, giving Hussein one last chance to disarm and authorizing a new team of weapons inspectors to search for weapons in Iraq. The team, called the UN Monitoring, Verification and Inspection Commission (UNMOVIC), begins inspections in late November 2002.

2003

January UNMOVIC and the International Atomic Energy Agency (IAEA) report to the UN that they had received access to Iraqi facilities but that no weapons of mass destruction had been discovered. Subsequent reports by Blix in February and March make similar reports.

February 24 The United States, Britain, and Spain circulate a second UN resolution to authorize war against Iraq, but it did not pass due to opposition from countries such as France, Germany, Russia, and China.

March 17 Bush announces the U.S. war plans in a speech to the nation.

March 19 The war begins with a missile strike on targets in Baghdad believed to be the command post for Saddam Hussein.

March 21 The air and land campaign against Iraq begins.

March 24 Saddam Hussein appears on Iraqi television and defiantly urges Iraqis to fight.

April 2 U.S. special operations forces rescue army private Jessica Lynch.

April 5 A group of American tanks rolls through Baghdad.

April 7 American bombers drop bombs on a compound in Baghdad, seeking to kill Hussein and his top leadership.

April 9 Iraqi citizens and U.S. Marines topple a statue of Saddam Hussein in Baghdad.

April 15 The U.S. Pentagon says the main fighting in Iraq is finished and President Bush declares that "the regime of Saddam Hussein is no more." Thereafter, looting erupts throughout Iraq. U.S. forces hold a meeting with various Iraqi political groups to discuss forming a provisional government for Iraq.

April 28 On Saddam Hussein's sixty-sixth birthday, a second meeting of Iraqi political groups decides to hold a national conference in May to select a "transitional government" for Iraq.

April 30 A newspaper prints a handwritten letter said to be written and signed by Saddam Hussein, urging Iraqis to rebel against the invaders.

May 12 Garner is fired and is replaced by a civilian administrator, L. Paul Bremer III, who initiates a tougher security policy to crack down on looting and policies to prevent Baath Party officials from holding government jobs.

May 16 Bremer reverses U.S. plans and announces that the coalition would remain in charge of Iraq for an indefinite period.

May 22 The UN Security Council votes unanimously to allow the United States and Britain to occupy and rebuild Iraq and to end economic sanctions.

June 2 Bremer meets with Iraqi political groups and promises to hold a national conference in July to create an interim Iraqi political council, which would be under U.S. authority.

May–June U.S. officials and American reconstruction contractors work to restore order, repair electrical and other utilities, and get Iraqi oil flowing.

July 22 Acting on a tip, U.S. troops locate and kill Saddam Hussein's two sons, Qusai and Odai.

August 19 A bomb attack destroys UN headquarters in Baghdad, kills the UN's special representative in Iraq (Segio Vieira de Mello) and seventeen others, and wounds one hundred more.

August 29 A bomb blast outside an Islamic shrine kills Ayatollah Mohammed Bakir al-Hakim, leader of the Supreme Council for Islamic Revolution in Iraq.

For Further Reading

Books

Fred Bratman, *War in the Persian Gulf.* Brookfield, CT: Millbrook, 1991. This is a young adult selection that discusses the 1990–1991 Persian Gulf crisis, from the Iraqi invasion of Kuwait in 1990 to the allied victory in 1991.

Joseph Braude, *The New Iraq: Rebuilding the Country for Its People, the Middle East, and the World.* New York: Basic Books, 2003. This book describes the effects of wars, sanctions, and Saddam Hussein's rule on Iraq's economy and the challenges that lie ahead for the postwar reconstruction of the country.

Richard Butler, *The Greatest Threat.* New York: PublicAffairs, 2000. This book is written by the head of the United Nations weapons inspection team that searched Iraq for weapons of mass destruction during the 1990s. It discusses that effort and the team's findings.

Paul J. Deegan, *Saddam Hussein.* Edina, MN: Abdo & Daughters, 1990. This is a young adult book that examines the life of Saddam Hussein.

Leila Merrell Foster, *Iraq.* New York: Childrens Press, 1998. This is a book written for young readers describing the geography, history, culture, industry, and people of Iraq.

Periodicals

Michael Duffy, "Weapons of Mass Disappearance: The War in Iraq Was Based Largely on Intelligence About Banned Arms That Still Haven't Been Found. Was America's Spy Craft Wrong—or Manipulated?" *Time,* June 9, 2003.

Earth Island Journal, "The Cost of War," Summer 2003.

Adnan R. Khan, "Killing Was Just a Game: Hundreds of Iraqis Are Digging Through Mass Graves in Search of Relatives," *Maclean's,* June 2, 2003.

Max Singer, "The Chalabi Factor," *National Review,* April 14, 2003.

Kevin Whitelaw and Mark Mazzetti, "Law and Disorder," *U.S. News & World Report,* May 26, 2003.

Websites

Iraq Action Coalition (http://leb.net/IAC). An online media and activists' resource center for groups and activists who opposed the war in Iraq.

The Iraq Foundation (www.iraqfoundation. org). A nonprofit, nongovernmental organization working for democracy and human rights in Iraq.

The Nonviolence Web, Iraq Crisis Anti-War Homepage (www.nonviolence. org). Home to dozens of major U.S. peace groups, with articles and information about postwar Iraq.

United Nations, Office of the Iraq Programme Oil-for-Food (www. un.org/Depts/oip). A UN website providing information about the oil-for-food program established by Security Council Resolution 986 in 1995.

U.S. Central Intelligence Agency (CIA) (www.cia.gov/cia/publications/fact book). A government website providing geographical, political, economic, and other information on the country of Iraq.

U.S. Department of State, International Information Programs (http://usinfo. state.gov/regional/nea/iraq). A government website providing information about current political issues and human rights involving Iraq.

Works Consulted

Books

Said K. Aburish, *Saddam Hussein, The Politics of Revenge.* New York: Bloomsbury, 2000. This is a biography of Saddam Hussein covering his rise to power and his reign as president of Iraq.

Con Coughlin, *Saddam: King of Terror.* New York: HarperCollins, 2002. This book traces the life of Saddam Hussein from his humble origins to his actions as leader of Iraq on the world stage, based on information from Western intelligence and interviews with Iraqi defectors.

Dilip Hiro, *The Longest War: The Iran-Iraq Military Conflict.* New York: Routledge Chapman & Hall, 1991. This is an easily readable account of the war between Iraq and Iran during the years between 1980 and 1988.

Helen Chapin Metz, ed., *Iraq, A Country Study.* Washington, DC: Library of Congressj 1988. http://memory.loc.gov. This is a Library of Congress study and report on Iraq, providing a good overview of its history, society, economy, government, military, and foreign policy.

Geoff Simons, *Iraq: From Sumer to Saddam.* New York: St. Martin's, 1994. This book provides a broad history of Iraq from ancient times to the present, with a particular focus on twentieth-century events.

Periodicals

Edmund L. Andrews, "Iraq Sanctions Lifted; Little Relief Expected," *New York Times,* May 23, 2003.

Edmund L. Andrews and Susan Sachs, "Iraq's Slide into Lawlessness Squanders Good Will for U.S.," *New York Times,* May 17, 2003.

R.W. Apple Jr., "Bush Moves to Prepare Public for a Harder War," *New York Times,* March 24, 2003.

Associated Press, "Bush Warns Allies Against Inaction in Confronting Baghdad," January 21, 2003.

———, "Parial Count Finds Many Civilians Killed," *San Diego Union-Tribune,* June 11, 2003.

Brian Bennett, "Sorting the Bad from the Not So Bad: To Get Iraq Back on Its Feet, the U.S. Needs Help from Officials of the Former Regime. But Which Ones Are Tolerable?" *Time,* May 19, 2003.

John M. Broder, "'Today the Regime Is in Disarray,' U.S. Commander Says," *New York Times,* April 9, 2003.

Business Week, "Whose Fuel Is in U.S. Cars? Increasingly, It's from Iraq," June 2002.

Lynette Clemetson, "Thousands in D.C. Protest Iraq War Plans," *New York Times,* January 20, 2003.

Maureen Dowd, "History up in Smoke," *New York Times,* April 16, 2003.

Jim Dwyer, "A Gulf Commander Sees a Longer Road," *New York Times,* March 28, 2003.

Economist (US), "The Other Battle; Humanitarian Assistance," April 5, 2003.

Dexter Filkins, "Hunting Hussein, U.S. Attacks Mosque." *New York Times,* April 11, 2003.

Thomas L. Friedman, "Because We Could," *New York Times*, June 4, 2003.

———, "Iraq Fast Becoming Yesterday's Story," *New York Times*, May 22, 2003.

———, "Our New Baby," *New York Times*, May 12, 2003.

David R. Gergen, "It's Time to Speak Loudly," *U.S. News & World Report*, August 19, 2002.

Joshua Hammer and Colin Soloway, "Who's in Charge Here? The First American Team Leading Iraq Was Plagued by Inexperience, Bureaucratic Infighting and Inertia," *Newsweek*, May 26, 2003.

Warren Hoge, "A Letter Said to Be from Saddam Hussein Urges Iraqis to Rebel," *New York Times*, April 30, 2003.

John B. Judis, "Below the Beltway: Between Iraq and a Hard Place," *American Prospect*, March 25, 2002.

Adnan R. Khan, "The Edge of Anarchy: To Slow Iraq's Drift into Total Chaos, the U.S. Changes Its Administration in the Country," *Maclean's*, May 26, 2003.

Rami G. Khouri, "Getting It Right in Iraq: Young Arabs Want Democratic Governments of Their Own Making," *Maclean's*, May 19, 2003.

Charlie LeDuff and David Rohde, "Turkey Says It Won't Send More Troops into Iraq," *New York Times*, March 26, 2003.

Melinda Liu, Rod Nordland, and Evan Thomas, "The Saddam Files," *Newsweek*, April 28, 2003.

Christopher Marquis, "World's View of U.S. Sours After Iraq War, Poll Finds," *New York Times*, June 4, 2003.

Judith Miller, "Iraqi Tells of Renovations at Sites for Chemical and Nuclear Arms," *New York Times*, December 20, 2001.

Terence Neilan, "Bremer Says U.S. Is Tackling Security Problem in Baghdad," *New York Times*, May 15, 2003.

New York Times, "A New War," March 24, 2003.

———, "Interview with Jacques Chirac," September 9, 2002.

———, "The Iraq Money Tree," April 14, 2003.

———, "The Quest for Illicit Weapons," April 18, 2003.

Stanley Reed, "How to Get Iraq's Economy on the Mend," *Business Week*, May 26, 2003.

Reuters, "Red Cross Urges U.S. to Secure Baghdad's Hospitals," April 11, 2003.

Frank Rich, "And Now: 'Operation Iraqi Looting,'" *New York Times*, April 28, 2003.

William Safire, "Clear Ties of Terror," *New York Times*, January 27, 2003.

David E. Sanger, "Viewing the War as a Lesson to the World," *New York Times*, April 5, 2003.

David E. Sanger and Thom Shanker, "Bush Says Regime in Iraq Is No More; Syria Is Penalized," *New York Times*, April 15, 2003.

Marc Santora, "From Hussein, Defiance and Praise for His Troops," *New York Times*, March 24, 2003.

Eric Schmitt, "Senators Sharply Criticize Iraq Rebuilding Efforts," *New York Times*, May 22, 2003.

Brent Scowcroft, "Don't Attack Saddam," *Wall Street Journal*, August 15, 2002.

Marlise Simons, "In the Street, Across Europe, a Weekend of Antiwar Rallies," *New York Times*, January 20, 2003.

David Stout, "U.S. Uncertain Whether Air Strike on Baghdad Got Hussein," *New York Times*, March 20, 2003.

Sabrina Tavernise, "Returning to Iraq, Few Kurds Want to Be Part of It," *New York Times*, May 24, 2003.

Patrick E. Tyler, "An Open Secret Is Laid Bare at Mass Grave in Iraqi Marsh," *New York Times*, May 15, 2003.

———, "In Reversal, Plan for Iraq Self-Rule Has Been Put Off," *New York Times*, May 15, 2003.

———, "Opposition Groups to Help to Create Assembly in Iraq," *New York Times*, May 5, 2003.

———, "U.S. Tanks Make Quick Strike into Baghdad," *New York Times*, April 6, 2003.

Douglas Waller, "Did the U.S. Betray Iraqis in 1991?" *Time*, April 14, 2003.

Andrew West, "800 Missiles to Hit Iraq in First 48 Hours," *Sun-Herald*, January 26, 2003.

Stephen Zunes, "Foreign Policy by Catharsis: The Failure of U.S. Policy Toward Iraq," *Arab Studies Quarterly*, Fall 2001.

Internet Sources

George W. Bush, Address to a Joint Session of Congress and the Nation, Washington, DC, September 20, 2001. www.whitehouse.gov.

———, President's State of the Union Address, Washington, DC, January 29, 2002. www.whitehouse.gov.

———, radio address to the nation, April 5, 2003. www.cbsnews. com.

———, remarks at MacDill Air Force Base Florida, March 26, 2003. www.white house.gov.

———, remarks at the Pentagon, Washington, DC, March 25, 2003. www.whitehouse.gov.

———, speech to the nation, January 3, 2003. www.whitehouse.gov.

———, speech to the United Nations, New York, September 12, 2002. www.white house.gov.

Osama bin Laden, speech made in a video-tape aired on Arabic television news network Al-Jazeera, October 7, 2001, September 11. News.com.

Richard Butler, Statement at the Senate Foreign Relations Committee, Washington, DC, July 31, 2002. www.iraqwatch.org.

Dick Cheney, speech at the American Society of Newspaper Editors, New Orleans, April 9, 2003. www.command-post. org.

———, speech to the Veterans of Foreign Wars 103rd National Convention, August 26, 2002. www.whitehouse. gov.

CNN, "Cheney: 'Time Is Not on Our Side,'" March 16, 2003. www.cnn.com.

———, "European Protesters Fill Cities," February 15, 2003. www.cnn.com.

Draft Resolution on Iraq by the United States, Great Britain, and Spain, circulated to the UN Security Council on February 23, 2003. www.cnn.com.

Al Gore, speech to the Commonwealth Club, San Francisco, September 9, 2002. www.gore2004us.com.

International Atomic Energy Agency, World Atom, Status of the Agency's Verification Activities in Iraq as of 8 January 2003, January 9, 2003. www. iaea.org.

Memo submitted to United Nations Security Council by France, Germany, and Russia on February 24, 2003. www. cnn.com.

Colin Powell, speech to the United Nations, New York, February 5, 2003. www.state. gov.

Resolution 1441, adopted by the United Nations at Security Council meeting 4644, November 8, 2002. www.cnn.com.

The White House, "A Decade of Deception and Defiance," September 12, 2002.

http://usinfo.state.gov.United Nations, United Nations Monitoring, Verification and Inspection Commission, Notes for Briefing the Security Council, January 9, 2003. www.un.org.

Index

Aburish, Said K., 17
Afghanistan, 30
   "coalition of the willing" and, 42
   terrorism and, 33
Albania, 42
allies
   air power of, 25
   "coalition of willing" and, 42
   criticize U.S., 34–35
   Gulf War and, 24–25
   Operation Iraqi Freedom and, 46
   troop support from, 72–73
America. *See* United States
anthrax, 31
Apache helicopters, 49
Arabs, 14, 16–17
   antiwar protests and, 36
   "coalition of willing" and, 42
   criticize U.S., 34–35
   Gulf War and, 24–25
   Kurdish property and, 86–87
   provisional government and, 75–76
Associated Press, 61
Atta, Mohamed, 33
Australia, 42
axis of evil, 28–34
Azerbaijan, 42
Aziz, Tariq, 55

Baath Party, 17
   banned from public office, 70
   Command Council of, 21
   economic effects of, 79
   employment and, 82
   increased membership of, 20
   Khomeini and, 22
   militia of, 49
   preventing resurgence of, 83–85
   search for members of, 53, 55
   violence of, 18–19

Baghdad, 33
   air strikes on, 46
   British invasion of, 16
   employment and, 82
   falls to U.S., 43, 49–53
   hospitals in, 65
   National Museum looting and, 66–67
   protests in, 77
   red zone around, 51
Baghdad Division, 51
Baradei, Mohamed El, 38
Basra, 16, 47, 63, 84
Bechtel, 79
bin Laden, Osama, 33, 40
Blair, Tony, 35
Blix, Hans, 37, 38
Blount, Buford C., III, 52
bombs, 10, 45, 55, 60
   suicide bombers and, 59, 82
Bremer, L. Paul, III
   appointment of, 70
   assessment of Iraq, 71
   Baath Party and, 84
   economic rebuilding and, 82–83
   interim government issues and, 76–79
Britain, 11, 23, 41, 89
   Afghanistan attack and, 30
   antiwar protests and, 36
   Baghdad attack and, 46
   "coalition of the willing" and, 42
   humanitarian aid and, 66
   Iraq creation and, 14, 16–17
   Operation Iraqi Freedom and, 46
   provisional government and, 76–77
   Resolution 1441 and, 37–38
   supports U.S., 35
British Petroleum, 21
Brooks, Vincent K., 53
Bulgaria, 42, 72
Bush, George H.W., 24

Bush, George W., 10
  arms inspections and, 25
  axis of evil and, 30–31
  "coalition of the willing" and, 41–42
  criticism of, 31, 33, 58
  declares war, 41–42
  diplomatic approach of, 35, 37
  humanitarian aid and, 66
  preemption and, 33, 58
  reports on length of war, 50
  "Shock and Awe" program and, 43–59
  UN occupation approval and, 78–79
  war on terrorism and, 28–35
Butler, Richard, 31, 33

al-Chadrichy, Nasir, 77
Chalabi, Ahmad, 77–78
Chemical Ali, 55
Cheney, Dick, 31, 43, 53
China, 41, 58
Chirac, Jacques, 35
Central Intelligence Agency (CIA), 17
  Hussein/bin Laden and, 33
  information challenged, 40–41
  weapons of mass destruction and, 37, 58
civilian casualties, 60–62
Clinton, Bill, 34
"coalition of the willing," 41–42
collateral damage, 60
Colombia, 42
communism, 17
Compagnie Francaise des Petroles, 21
Coughlin, Con, 18, 23, 25
courts, 18
Czech Republic, 33, 42

Al Daawa al Islamiya, 21
Daawa Party, 77
de-Baathification, 85
democracy, 69, 75–77
Democrats, 31
Denmark, 42, 72

economic issues
  business investment and, 83

  Central Bank and, 79–80
  employment restoration and, 81–82
  food and, 62–64
  health care and, 65–66
  industry rebuilding and, 79–81
  Iran-Iraq war and, 23
  middle class and, 62
  oil and, 21
  postwar Iraq and, 11–13, 60–73
  UN sanctions and, 25–27
  war cost and, 12–13
Economist (magazine), 62–63
education, 74, 82
Egypt, 14–15, 17
El Salvador, 42, 72
employment, 81–82
Eritrea, 42
Esso, 21
Estonia, 42
Ethiopia, 42
ethnic issues, 74–75, 86–88
Euphrates River, 14–15

F-117 Nighthawks, 45
Faisal (king of Iraq), 16
fatwa (religious ruling), 78
Fischer, Joschka, 40–41
food, 26, 52–54, 62–64
France, 21, 23
  approves U.S. occupation, 78–79
  opposes war, 35, 41
Friedman, Thomas L., 13, 73–74

Garner, Jay, 70, 76
Geneva Conventions, 65
Georgia, 42
Gergen, David, 35
Germany
  approves U.S. occupation, 78–79
  opposes war, 35, 41
Gore, Al, 34
Greece, 15, 36
guerrillas, 47, 83–85
Gulf War, 24–25, 42–43, 88

Habbaniya, 69

al-Hakim, Abdul, 78
al-Hakim, Ayatollah Muhammad Bakr, 77, 88
Halabja, 87
Hassan, Karim W., 68
health care, 64–66
Honduras, 72
humanitarian aid, 52–54, 62–66, 68
Hungary, 42, 72
Hussein, Qusay, 55, 79–80
Hussein, Saddam
    attempts to kill, 43–45
    Baath Party and, 17
    business skills of, 83
    Daawa Party and, 21
    ethnic cleansing by, 86–87
    Gulf War and, 24–25
    Kuwait and, 23–24
    loyal fighters for, 46–53
    nepotism of, 20
    oil and, 21, 68
    refuses to leave, 41
    regime collapse of, 53
    regrouping of, 13
    removal of, 10, 28, 31, 33
    Republican Guard of, 46
    return of, 89
    rise of, 17–21
    Saddam Fedayeen and, 47
    search for, 53, 55
    seizes presidency, 21
    survival of, 84
    television appearances of, 45, 49, 52
    threatens scientists, 39–40
    toppled statue of, 10–11, 52–53
    violence of, 14, 18–19, 54, 69, 86–87
    weapons of mass destruction and, 32

India, 16
interim government, 76–77
International Atomic Energy Agency (IAEA),
    38, 41–42
International Committee of the Red Cross
    (ICRC), 63
Iran, 58
    as axis of evil, 30–31
    Khomeini and, 22

    Kurds and, 21
    war with Iraq and, 21–23
Iraq
    accused of noncooperation, 38–41
    ancient, 15
    as axis of evil, 30–31
    British creation of, 14, 16–17
    democracy and, 75–77
    employment restoration and, 81–82
    ethnic issues in, 74–75, 86–88
    future of, 88–89
    Gulf War and, 24–25
    health care and, 64–66
    humanitarian aid to, 52–54, 62–66, 68
    inspectors removed from, 41–42
    Iran war and, 21–23
    Kuwait attack and, 23–24
    looting in, 65–70, 79, 82
    postwar conditions in, 11–13, 60–73
    power vacuum in, 64, 66, 69–70
    provisional government for, 74–78, 88–89
    religion in, 14, 21, 36, 77–78, 86–88
    Resolution 1441 and, 37–38
    "Shock and Awe" program and, 43–59
    "smoking gun" and, 38–39
    terrorism links of, 33–34
    UN sanctions and, 25–27
    utility restoration and, 63–65, 68–69, 79, 83
    see also oil; weapons of mass destruction
Iraqi Intelligence Service, 84
Iraqi National Accord, 77
Iraqi National Congress, 77–78
Iraqi Oil Ministry, 67
Iraqi Petroleum Company (IPC), 21
Iraq War. *See* Operation Iraqi Freedom
Islam, 14, 21
Islamic Call, 21
Islamic Revolution, 21, 77–78, 88
Israel, 19
Italy, 42, 66

al-Janabi, Ali, 85
Japan, 42

al-Khoei, Abdel Majid, 88
Khomeini, Ayatollah, 22

Khouri, Rami G., 80
Kirkuk, 53, 87
Kohut, Andrew, 59
Kurds, 17, 27, 53
    ethnic violence and, 86–88
    independence for, 88
    property reclamation by, 86–87
    provisional government and, 75, 77
    Saddam Hussein's treatment of, 20–21, 23, 32
Kuwait
    Gulf War and, 23–25
    mass graves and, 69
    U.S. antimissile system and, 51

Latvia, 42
leadership council, 77–78
liberator role, 11, 13
Lithuania, 42
Liu, Melinda, 54
looting, 65–70, 79, 82
Lugar, Richard G., 73
Lynch, Jessica, 48

Macedonia, 42
Maclean's, (magazine) 80
Mahawil, 69
Mahdi, Adel Abdel, 77
al-Majid, Ali Hassan, 55
Mansur, 55
mass graves, 69
media, 18, 46
medicine, 63–66
Medina Division, 51
Mello, Sérgio Vieira de, 78
Mesopotamia, 14–15
military
    collateral damage and, 60–62
    guerrilla attacks and, 83–85
    increased troop numbers and, 70, 72–73
    long-term commitment of, 12–13
    Saddam Hussein and, 21
    "Shock and Awe" program, 43–59
    see also war
mines, 63
missiles, 10, 45
Mobil, 21

mobile labs, 57–58
Mohammad (prophet), 14
moral issues
    criticism of U.S., 10–12
    UN sanctions and, 25–26
Mosul, 53
Muslims. See Islam

Najaf, 49
Nasiriya, 47
National Museum, 66–67
nerve gas, 31
Netherlands, 42
Newsweek (magazine), 54
New York Times (newpaper), 13, 49, 58, 68, 73–74, 88
Nicaragua, 42
Nida Division, 51
no-fly zones, 27
nomads, 14
Nordland, Rod, 54
North Korea
    as axis of evil, 30–31
    changed position of, 58

Obeidi, Saad, 84
oil, 11, 21, 74, 77
    antiwar protests and, 36
    destruction of, 46
    for food, 26, 62–63
    industry reconstruction and, 79–81
    production rate of, 81
    protection of, 51, 67–68
    Rumeila field and, 80
    weapons and, 23
Operation Desert Fox, 27
Operation Desert Storm, 24–25, 27
Operation Desert Strike, 27
Operation Iraqi Freedom
    air strikes and, 46
    casualties and, 48–49, 60–62
    cost of, 65–66, 72
    fall of Baghdad and, 43, 49–53
    ground maneuvers and, 46
    guerrillas and, 47
    health care and, 64–66

humanitarian efforts and, 62–64
initial strike, 43–45
Iraqi resistance and, 43, 46–53
looting and, 65–70, 79, 82
Lynch and, 48
postwar chaos and, 66–72
profits from, 72, 79
psychological warfare and, 46
Saddam Hussein's fall and, 53, 55
search for Baath Party members and, 53, 55
unexpected length of, 50
U.S. reputation and, 58–59
U.S. troop size and, 49–50
victory declaration and, 53
weather obstacles, 49
Organization of Petroleum Exporting Countries (OPEC), 23
Ottoman rule, 16

peace
Iraq War's effect on, 58–59
postwar chaos and, 66–73
Perle, Richard, 31
Pew Research Center for the People and the Press, 59
Philippines, 42
playing cards (wanted posters), 55
Poland, 42
politics
axis of evil label and, 28–34
British occupation and, 14, 16–17
civilian casualties and, 60–62
"coalition of the willing" and, 41–42
democracy and, 69, 75–77
employment restoration and, 81–82
Islamic Revolution and, 21, 77–78, 88
leadership council and, 77
liberator role and, 11–13
no-fly zones and, 27
opposition to Iraqi policy and, 31, 33
preemption and, 33, 58
provisional government and, 74–78
Saddam Hussein and, 14, 18–21
"Shock and Awe" program and, 43–59
Sunnis and, 16–17
transitional government and, 76

unilateralism and, 34–35, 42
UN occupation approval and, 78–79
UN sanctions and, 25–27
war on terrorism and, 28–35
war profits and, 72, 79
weapons of mass destruction and, 55–58
see also specific political parties
Popular Army, 20
Powell, Colin, 33
"coalition of the willing" and, 42
criticizes Iraq, 38–40
"smoking gun" and, 38–39
preemption, 33, 58
propaganda, 20, 48, 72
psychological warfare, 46, 53

al-Qaeda, 28, 30, 33–34, 40
Qasim, Abdul Karim, 17
Al Quds al Arabi (newspaper), 55

Red Cross, 63, 65
red zone, 51
religion, 14, 74
antiwar protests and, 36
Daawa Party and, 21
ethnic violence and, 86–88
fatwa and, 78
Islamic Revolution and, 21, 77–78, 88
toleration and, 86–88
see also Shiites; Sunnis
Republican Guard, 46, 51, 84
Republicans, 31
Resolution 1441, 37–38, 41
Rich, Frank, 67–68
Romania, 42
Rome, 15
Rumeila oil field, 23, 80
Rumsfeld, Donald H., 45, 70
Russia, 23
approves U.S. occupation, 78–79
criticizes U.S., 35
opposes war, 36, 41

Saddam Fedayeen (Martyrs of Saddam), 47, 49, 84
"Saddam Files, The" (Newsweek), 54

Saddam: King of Terror (Coughlin), 18
al-Sadr, Moktada, 88
Salih, Barham, 88
Saudi Arabia, 23–24, 59
Sawers, John, 76–77
scientists, 39–40
security
    Bremer and, 70–71
    postwar chaos and, 66–73
Senate Foreign Relations Committee, 73
September 11, 2001, 28–30
Shell, 21
Shiites, 14
    British occupation and, 16–17
    Daawa Party and, 77
    ethnic violence and, 86–88
    Islamic Revolution and, 21, 77–78
    Khomeini and, 22
    mass graves of, 69
    neutrality of, 49
    provisional government and, 75
    revolt of, 16
    United States and, 27
"Shock and Awe" program
    air strikes, 46
    Baghdad and, 49–53
    ground strikes, 46
    initial strike, 43–45
    Iraqi resistance and, 46–50
    results of, 58–59
Simons, Geoff, 16–17, 19, 21
al-Sistani, Ayatollah Ali, 78
Slovakia, 42, 72
"smoking gun," 38–39
South Korea, 42
Soviet Union, 23
Spain, 41–42, 66, 72
Special Republican Guard, 46
suicide bombings, 59, 82
Sultan, Jamal Mustafa Abdallah, 55
Sumer, 15, 67
Sunnis, 14
    Baath Party and, 17
    British occupation and, 16–17
    ethnic violence and, 86–88
    political domination by, 16–17

    provisional government and, 75
    revolt of, 16
Syria, 14, 16, 53, 57–58

Taliban, 30
terrorism
    axis of evil and, 30–31
    Baath Party and, 83–86
    Iraqi links to, 33–34
    Iraq War's effect on, 58–59
    al-Qaeda and, 28, 33
    Saddam Hussein and, 18
    September 11, 2001, 28–30
    suicide bombers and, 59, 82
Third Infantry Division, 52, 71
Thomas, Evan, 54
Tigris River, 14–15
Tikrit, 17, 53
al-Tikriti, Abid Hamid Mahmoud, 55
al-Tikriti, Barzan Ibrahim Hasan, 55
torture, 18–19, 54, 69, 86–87
Turkey, 17, 24, 36, 42
Tyler, Patrick E., 69

Ukraine, 72
Umm Qasr, 47, 49, 63
unilateralism, 34–35, 42
United Nations, 11–12, 59
    approves U.S. occupation, 78–79
    arms inspections by, 25–27, 37–42
    criticizes U.S., 34–35
    Gulf War and, 24–25
    Iran-Iraq war and, 23
    Iraqi noncooperation with, 38–41
    Kuwait attack and, 23–24
    Monitoring, Verification and Inspection
      Commission (UNMOVIC), 37–38, 41–42
    oil and, 26, 62–63, 80
    opposes war, 41
    Powell's address to, 32
    removes inspectors, 41–42
    Resolution 1441 and, 37–38, 41
    sanctions by, 25–27, 62, 78
    "smoking gun" and, 38–39
    Special Commission on Iraq (UNSCOM),
      25, 31

World Food Programme (WFP), 63
United States
    Afghanistan attack and, 30
    air strikes of, 25–27
    antiwar protests and, 36
    blamed for looting, 67–68
    Central Intelligence Agency, 17, 33, 37,
        40–41, 58
    "coalition of the willing" and, 41–42
    criticism of, 10–13, 27, 34–35, 58, 73
    declares victory, 53
    declares war, 41–42
    Gulf War and, 24–25, 42–43, 88
    humanitarian aid and, 63, 66
    Iran-Iraq war and, 23
    as liberator, 11–13
    military strength of, 10
    nation-building policy of, 12–13
    postwar chaos and, 69–73
    preemption and, 33, 58
    provisional government and, 74–78, 88–89
    Resolution 1441 and, 37–38, 41
    September 11, 2001 and, 28–30
    "Shock and Awe" program, 43–59
    "smoking gun" and, 38–39
    Third Infantry Division, 52, 71
    transitional government and, 76
    unilateralism of, 34–35, 42
    UN occupation approval and, 78–79
Ur (Sumerian city), 15, 67
Uthman, Mahmoud Ahmed, 66
utilities, 63–65, 68–69, 79, 83
Uzbekistan, 42

Villepin, Dominique de, 40–41
violence
    ethnic, 86–88
    mass graves and, 69
    Saddam Hussein and, 14, 18–19, 54
    torture, 18–19, 54
    see also war

Wallace, William, 49–50
war
    antiwar protests and, 36
    civilian casualties and, 60–62

cost of, 12–13
    declaration of, 41–42
    Geneva Conventions and, 65
    Gulf War, 24–25, 42–43, 88
    Iran-Iraq, 21–23
    preemption and, 33, 58
    profiting from, 72, 79
    psychological, 46, 53
    religion and, 21, 77–78, 88
    Resolution 1441 and, 37–38, 41
    "Shock and Awe" program, 43–59
    World War I, 16
    see also specific operations
water, 52–54
weapons
    anthrax, 31
    Baath Party and, 83–84
    ban on assault, 70
    biological, 23, 26, 57–58
    bombs, 10, 45, 55, 59–60, 82
    chemical, 23, 25, 55–58
    increase of, 59
    mines, 63
    missiles, 45, 51
    nerve gas, 31
    nuclear, 23, 25, 31–32
    Resolution 1441 and, 37–38
    seizure of, 83–85
    "smoking gun" and, 38–39
    UN inspections and, 25–27, 37–41
weapons of mass destruction, 11
    Bush policy and, 31, 33
    evidence for, 32
    failure to find, 38–39, 41, 80
    mobile labs and, 57–58
    search for, 25–27, 37–41, 55–58
    secret disposal of, 56–57
    "smoking gun" and, 38–39
Win Without War (coalition), 36
Wolfowitz, Paul D., 31, 73
World Health Organization, 63, 65–66
World Trade Center, 29
World War I, 16

al-Zarqawi, Abu Musaab, 33, 40
Zobeidi, Muhammad Mohsen, 70

Picture Credits

About the Author

Debra Miller is a writer and lawyer with an interest in current events and history. She began her law career in Washington, D.C., where she worked on legislative, policy, and legal matters in government, public interest, and private law firm positions. She now lives with her husband in Encinitas, California. She has written and edited numerous publications for legal publishers, as well as books and anthologies on historical and political topics.